BIG IDEAS... FOR
SMALL BUSINESSES

SIMPLE, PRACTICAL TOOLS AND TACTICS TO
HELP YOUR SMALL BUSINESS GROW

JOHN LAMERTON

LET'S TELL YOUR STORY
PUBLISHING

COPYRIGHT

For Linda. Miss you, Sis.

CONTENTS

ACKNOWLEDGEMENTS

This is the part of the book that most people skim over, unless you know the author personally, in which case you'll read it line-by-line to see if I've remembered to namecheck you. If I have, you're welcome – and if I haven't, I'm sure it was an honest oversight.

So, a big thank you, thank you, thank you...

To you, dear reader for investing in your education by buying this book. I really hope it makes a difference in your life – if it does, please let me know (john@bigidea.co.uk) as hearing about people making positive changes to their lives makes me feel ten feet tall for the day, as do five-star Amazon reviews, and cake (I can be bribed with either!).

To Sarah, for holding everything together whilst I took time out of our lives to write "this bloody book" as it became known by the end. To Jack and Harry for putting up with me being Grumpy Dad (and getting grumpier the closer I got to deadline...) – I owe you guys, BIG time, and I'm coming back down your end of the see-saw right now.

To Jason, for being my right hand man for the last 14 years. I think it's safe to say we've done alright. Thanks for taking the load whilst I focused on this book. I don't do well spinning multiple plates, and the only reason I can do so well focusing on my one spinning plate is knowing that I've got you following me around, furiously keeping all the other plates from crashing to the ground.

To my friends and family. It's been 17 years now, and many of you STILL don't know what I do (don't worry Dad, I haven't included the story about you trying to stick stamps on emails...), but you've kept me grounded, and always supported me, and for that I'll be eternally grateful.

To the rest of the Big Idea team – Rob, Joe, Mel, Stu, Matt, Alice, Sarah, and Kayliegh for ensuring that I still had a business to return to whilst I took time away from my desk to write this book.

To my peers and mentors – Clarke, Jason D, Thom, Andy, Mark, Seb, Damian, Julia, Phil, Keith, Pete, Jo, Lucy, Dave, Ed, James, Nigel, Siam, Terry, Jason V, Rob M, Rob B, Rob D (how many Robs?!), Tim, and Tracy. I've spent a lot of time with some of you, a chance conversation, or a brief meeting with others – but you've all impacted my life in such a way that, when it came to writing the acknowledgements section of my book, I thought of you. It's a cliché, but I really wouldn't be who I am today without you.

To everyone who helped turn this book into a reality – Lee from LCG Design for the amazing cover design, Keith, Rupert, Sharon, Kirry, Matt, Simon and Jo for beta reading (and there were a LOT of typos in the original I can tell you!). Tracy, Nigel, Tim, Terry, Jo, and Dave for providing stories, anecdotes, ideas and sayings that I've used throughout the book. If I've said something funny or inspiring in this book, it's probably thanks to one of these guys. Thanks to Colette for turning my final draft into a published book.

To everyone who helped with the marketing of the book (something I neglected until I'd actually finished writing the damn thing!) – Mark, Mike T, Thom, Hannah, Dan, Lucy, Bracken, Mike K.

To Warren – we've never met, and likely never will, but on the off-chance you read this, I want to thank you for being you. You're an inspiration to me – whenever I have a decision to make (business, investment, or personal), the answer usually comes to me when I ask myself these five words – "What would Warren Buffett do?"

INTRODUCTION – TO HELL WITH HUSTLE...

"I hate being busy. I'm the laziest ambitious person I know."

Tim Kreider

I've been running small businesses since the year 2000 – some successful, some not. But I've learned a shed-load of really useful stuff along the way. And there are some common traits amongst the successful businesses that I've created – traits that just about anyone can put into practice to take their business to the next level (regardless of what level you're currently at)

I've hired staff, fired staff, taken people to court, made a million quid, lost a million quid, sold businesses, bought businesses, laid awake at night worrying about paying the bills, feeling totally overwhelmed. At times I've wanted to jack it all in and get a "real" job, and at other times I've felt on top of the world like everything I touch turns to gold.

It's a safe bet that if you're struggling with any aspect of your business right now, I've probably lived through that myself at some point over the last two decades.

I'm a former civil servant, who quit the day job back in 2001 to chase a dream of becoming an internet millionaire. Despite not even owning a computer, let alone having access to the Internet on it, or knowing anything about web design, internet marketing, or... erm... how to actually run a business.

And yet I DID become an internet millionaire. Granted, I didn't manage to KEEP many of those millions, but I DID earn them! Nowadays, I run several companies in the sports betting and property sectors and mentor ambitious lifestyle business owners. Oh, and I still do some stuff on the internet . I've stopped chasing the dream of "making millions" now though, and started "living like a millionaire" instead (more on this in the next chapter).

I wrote this book to share some of the simple, practical ways to grow a small business that I've picked up over the last couple of decades. If you're looking for the latest "silver bullet" techniques that involve creating a "funnel" the size of a cross-channel ferry, you're going to be disappointed.

If you want to know how to "blow up" your startup, turn it into a "unicorn", and exit for £50m three years from now, then this book ain't gonna be for you. Likewise if you're a big fan of the "grind", or "hustle" as our American cousins like to call it – if working three days straight without sleep, or surviving on a diet of coffee and cigarettes is a badge of honour for you, I'll save you some precious time right now – put this book down and go back to hustling / grinding / getting shit done / JFDI'ing / some other fancy term for "working really, really hard, for a really, really long time".

Don't get me wrong. I like to "get shit done" as much as the next guy, but I like to get the RIGHT shit done. Not any old shit. Why "hustle" for 100 hours a week doing the wrong stuff, when you could do the things that REALLY move your business forward in 20 to 25 hours a week, and spend the rest of the time with your family, friends, on the golf course, sailing, at the gym, looking at cat videos on the internet , or whatever else floats your boat?

I mentor ambitious lifestyle business owners, and this book is for them. Don't instantly turn your nose up because I used the term "lifestyle business" – I've never really understood the disregard that so many people have for lifestyle businesses. I'm forever hearing people say things like "oh, they'll only ever be a lifestyle business", or "oh, they're not a real business, they're just a lifestyle business".

I'm not talking about someone who's pursuing a hobby and dressing it up as a business. I'm talking about owners of small businesses who have ambition, drive, a desire to grow and succeed, but who also want their small business to provide them with a certain lifestyle. And they can DESIGN their business to do exactly that. This is where this book can help. So if you're a small business owner, and your business isn't currently giving you the lifestyle you want, then:

1.   That's YOUR fault

2.   You CAN change it

3.   This book can HELP you do so

What this book covers

There are five broad topics that we'll cover in this book – I call them my "magic ingredients", partly because I believe they can make any ambitious lifestyle business successful (but mainly because I can't think of a better name for them!).

I'll introduce you to these "magic ingredients" in chapter three, and all subsequent chapters roughly follow these five themes – but they also serve as standalone lessons on their own merits.

The five magic ingredients are:

1. Goals

2. Desire

3. Knowledge

4. Environment

5. Action

Some of the other "BIG IDEAs" you'll learn from reading this book include:

- How almost ANYONE could become a millionaire in their lifetime, given just £200 a month
- Why I blame Richard Branson for my early failures
- How to sell a dozen eggs for over £500
- The ONE THING that truly transformed my business
- How I told fear to f*** off
- EXACTLY how I made over £100k from ONE marketing campaign
- What the death of my sister taught me about purpose
- How I earn more money working 20 to 25 hours a week than I did working 100+ per week
- How I juggle running an ambitious lifestyle business with raising two young children

How to use this book

I've deliberately kept things simple in this book – I hate it when some internet marketing "guru" comes along, and dresses up something that's pretty basic to make it look really complex, just so he looks clever. If you're aspiring to be the next Elon Musk or Richard Branson, then you probably do need to learn some pretty complex stuff, but for the rest of us mere mortals, running a successful, ambitious lifestyle business isn't that hard, and needn't be that complex.

This book is written to be semi-autobiographical, so I've used several stories from the last 17 years of my business career, and a couple from my previous life as a civil servant. They say a wise man learns from his mistakes, whilst a genius learns from someone else's mistakes – well, here's your chance to learn from mine – because believe me, I've made some crackers in my time.

With the benefit of hindsight, I can now see why I failed so spectacularly at times. Hopefully, I'll be able to stop one or two of you from making those same mistakes. Of course, I've also had quite a few successes in that time too, and there are plenty of examples, tools and tactics that you can swipe and deploy in your business.

It's my aim that whatever stage you're at in your small business career, this book will give you at least a handful of big questions to ask yourself about the way you operate and the lifestyle that your business is currently giving you. I hope it'll make you laugh at times; it may make you cry at others, but more than anything I hope it makes you THINK.

Alongside the narrative, detailing the rollercoaster ride that has been my first two decades as a small business owner, you'll find my "big ideas" – these are the key lessons that I would like you to take away from reading this book. Some of them are clichés. Some of them you'll have heard before.

Every single one of them has positively impacted either my business, my life, or both at some point. They're all simple, practical tools and tactics that you can begin to deploy in your business the minute you finish reading this book, and every one of them has the potential to help your business grow.

Let's go!

There are loads more nuggets than that to be found in the next couple of hundred pages, but I don't want to give you too many spoilers and ruin your appetite. Are you ready to dive in? Great – so let's look at exactly WHY I'm so passionate about ambitious lifestyle businesses.

WHY DO PEOPLE HATE LIFESTYLE BUSINESSES?

*"Do your kids remember you for being the best dad?
Not the dad who gave them everything, but will they
be able to tell you anything one day? Will they be able
to call you, out of the blue, any day, no matter what?
Are you the first person they want to ask for advice?*

*And at the same time, can you hit it out of the park in
whatever it is you decide to do, as a lawyer, as a
doctor, as a stockbroker, as a whatever?"*

Peter Attia

Why are you in business?

What made you decide that working for yourself, being your own boss was a good idea?

Was it to "make millions"?

Was it to get a massive house in the country, supercars in your garage and supermodels in your bed?

Or maybe something less "arsehole-y" than that?

If you were to sit down right now and write your ultimate job description – literally, suspend reality, what would be the ideal role for you? Now ask yourself what effect this role could have on your life.

I went through this exercise myself, and ended up writing myself the following job description:

"To do what I want, where I want, how I want, when I want.

If I want..."

That VERY clearly defines what I want from my business. So my business now has just ONE purpose...

TO PROVIDE ME WITH THE LIFESTYLE I WANT.

Total freedom to choose whether to work or not. To be in total control of WHAT I work on. To be able to work from ANYWHERE in the world. To do things MY way.

That's the lifestyle I want – and I can now design my business to provide that lifestyle.

What lifestyle do YOU want?

Maybe you want to earn £100k a year?

Maybe you want to spend more time with friends and family, or travel more?

You might want to give up the day job, or completely change direction in your business.

Perhaps you want to retire in 2 / 5 / 10 years?

Remove yourself from doing the jobs you HATE?

Sack your problem clients?

Sack all your staff, close the offices and become a digital nomad?

Shut down the business and do something you TRULY love instead?

I truly believe that if you are a majority shareholder in your business, then you have a lifestyle business – the choices you make, and the way you run your business ultimately dictate the lifestyle that you and your family will enjoy.

Lifestyle businesses are real businesses

So why then are so many people so disparaging about lifestyle businesses? I used to watch the first few series of the TV show Dragons' Den, where business owners would pitch their ideas to a panel of angel investors. 'Er Indoors has since banned me from watching it, as I start getting angry and shouting at the telly whenever it's on.

One of the main things about that show that gets my blood pressure rising, apart from the formulaic approach, the endless procession of crackpot inventors at the expense of actual small business owners, the clueless people pitching crap ideas, and people valuing their idea (having sold precisely zero units) at a million quid, was the way certain "dragons" looked down their nose at lifestyle business owners.

Almost every week, a small business owner would be paraded in front of the investors, explain that they've started up a small business making jam, or hand-crafted products. They'd be made to feel inferior to the uber-wealthy dragons, who would sneer at them, ridicule them for not wearing a pinstripe suit, accuse the poor person pitching of wasting their valuable time, and then dismiss them with a wave of their hand, and some variation of the line "This will only ever be a lifestyle business, it's not a real business... I'm out."

So any wannabe ambitious lifestyle business owners watching this primetime TV program for inspiration will hear that line time and time again – "lifestyle businesses are not real businesses."

Bollocks.

Utter bollocks.

I've heard it myself, when at a networking event – I've explained what I do, how I work, and (most importantly) why I choose to run an ambitious lifestyle business. Only to then be told, "Well, if you ever want to run a real business, you should talk to one of my VC (venture capital) mates." Who the hell is this person to tell me that I'm not running a "real" business? The last time I checked, my "little lifestyle business" has paid my bills for the last two decades, enabled me to travel the world, currently employs seven members of staff, owns a number of properties throughout the UK, and helps to mentor the next generation of ambitious lifestyle business owners.

Hell, imagine what I could have done if I'd been running a "real" business!

No really, let's just imagine for a second...

I could own less than half of my company.

I could owe millions to VCs, banks and angel investors.

I could have an army of accountants in pinstripe suits telling me how to run my own business. I could be told where I have to have offices, how many people I have to employ, what markets I need to go into, what products I need to sell, how I need to market them.

I could work 100+ hour weeks again and spend no time with my children.

Remember my dream job description?

> To do what I want, where I want, how I want, when I want... if I want...

Real business or nightmare role?

Well, it looks like running a "real" business would be my nightmare job description!

Don't get me wrong, I'm not saying that NOBODY should ever seek investment in their businesses, or take VC money etc. If the lifestyle YOU want is £30m in the bank, to work your arse off for a few years so that you never have to work again, the VC route is probably your best bet. But it's also just as likely to see you flat on your arse, burned out, and abandoned by your friends and family.

It never fails to amaze me when I see startup entrepreneurs who have never sold a single product to anyone who wasn't their mum, congratulated by their peers for securing funding, as though they'd actually gone out and sold their business and pocketed that money. You'd certainly think they had if you'd seen them spending their investors' money on Moet & Chandon and hookers as they celebrate being a "successful entrepreneur" by borrowing half a million quid of someone else's money.

Too many entrepreneurs these days seem to think that the sole purpose of their first six months in business is to get investment, at which point they'll then focus on the next important milestone – the second round of investment! The only skill the VC seeker ever learns is how to borrow and spend other people's money. By contrast, the ambitious lifestyle business owner learns how to sell their products, and make a profit – because if they don't, the kids don't get fed. Stuff like that can really motivate you to shift a lot of products!

Profit is more important than turnover

The success of a business can only be measured by the bottom line (net profit) – it cannot be measured by the top line (turnover). Yet so many celebrity entrepreneurs brag about the huge turnovers they have, as if the sheer volume of cash that they watched flow through their company was something to be impressed with.

You can just imagine them sitting in their expensive Mayfair offices, laughing uncontrollably as they watch all that lovely cash just washing through their company like a waterfall, without even realising that the flow of cash is not the same as the capture of profits. Watching millions flowing through your company and capturing 1% of it isn't that impressive.

An ambitious lifestyle business with one tenth of the turnover, yet which captures 10% of it as profit is exactly as successful (and less likely to fail, as they can afford a temporary hit to their margins). If you're making 1% or 2% on the cash flowing through your business, you HAVE to be as big as Tesco to make it work, and scale up massively, all the while dealing with transactional customers who have zero loyalty to you, and will immediately transfer their entire weekly spend to your fiercest rival if they can save 20p on a crate of beer.

By contrast, ambitious lifestyle businesses that compete on experience rather than price don't have to scale – they can make as much money as they want to, running things exactly as they want to, with one branch, one store, one restaurant. When you're making 30% or 40% net margins, you can be as big, or as small as you want to be.

The MLM brigade and the illusion of business

Another reason lifestyle businesses get dismissed as "not a real business" is due to the MLM brigade jumping on the bandwagon, and promoting their pyramid schemes as lifestyle businesses. Look at just about any sales page for any MLM product, and you'll see images of foreign travel, wealth, fast cars, and talk of "residual income", "passive income", and the opportunity to "run your own business around your lifestyle" – that sounds like a lifestyle business to me.

Only it's not.

BIG IDEA...

I believe the only way to truly own a lifestyle business is to be in complete control of the business – to be able to dictate how you work, when you work, where you work, what products you sell, what prices you charge, to be able to completely design the business around the lifestyle you want.

All you get with the MLM brigade is the illusion of a lifestyle business. You hear the success stories of the guys at the top who are driving around in their white Mercedes, having six foreign holidays a year, and who live in a nice detached "executive" home, all paid for by the one hour a day they work on "their business".

All of this is paid for by the hundreds, if not thousands of people below them in their "downline", who are just scraping by, pestering enough of their family and friends to buy their crap to earn a few quid. They're driving around in a rust-coloured 1998 Ford Mondeo, having a weekend in Skegness (sorry Skeggie – had to choose somewhere!) every year, and are struggling to pay the rent on their two-bed terrace in an ok-ish part of town.

And that's all paid for by their day job, as "their" MLM business is giving them bugger all except alienating them from all their friends and family – people don't want to take their calls anymore, cross the road if they see them in the street, and avoid chatting with them online, in case they start pestering them yet again about this bloody "fantastic opportunity" that they're forever trying to give the people who love them the hard sell on.

That's the reality of most MLM schemes. They sell you on white Mercedes and foreign holidays, paid for by doing a little, really easy work. And you end up with the 1998 Mondeo, sat in Skegness, wondering why your friends and family no longer take your calls...

MLM and me

I've worked with some MLM schemes before and even had some success. But only by doing what most MLM people don't do – by focusing on selling the products to people who are actually interested in buying them. Revolutionary! I was the top customer gatherer for one company every month for almost a year just by doing this, while everyone else was off pestering their work colleagues to buy some crap they neither wanted or needed – and then trying to recruit them to do the same.

One of the main tactics I used was Google Adwords – I'd target Google users who were searching for the products that this MLM company sold, send them to the website, and make sales. Pretty standard stuff – targeting people who WANT what you sell, and giving them the opportunity to buy it.

Last year I decided to see if I could resurrect that campaign, so I went through the latest online training for the MLM company. I could see there was a section on Google Adwords, so thought I'd start there, as it was going to be my main route to market, only to see the following advice being dished out:

"Using Google Adwords is forbidden. This type of anonymous, transactional marketing leads to the type of customer who doesn't pay their bill. Focus on talking to more of your friends and family instead."

What?

Really??

People who use Google don't pay bills? I've got over ten years' worth of commission statements (from the customers I referred via Google back in 2005 / 6) that would demonstrate otherwise.

 BIG IDEA...

"The whole world" is NOT your target market.

And here for me, lies the reason why "your" MLM business isn't actually a lifestyle business – you don't control the business. The MLM company will tell you how THEY want you to run it. They'll provide you with (normally pretty awful) marketing materials, and then tell you that you CAN'T use anything else. They'll give you a set script that you HAVE to follow. Want a yellow BMW rather than a white Merc? Tough shit.

Oh, and if you get the white Merc, and take some time off (maybe for one of those six foreign holidays you've planned), and find that your earnings have dropped below a certain level, that Merc still needs paying for – and guess whose name the lease is in? It sure as hell ain't the MLM company.

One I used to work with gave everyone who sold 200 products a Porsche Boxster for a month. This was genius marketing on their behalf, as nothing says living the lifestyle business dream like "Alright Dave, do you want to come out for a spin in my new Porsche? Oh yeah, it's a perk of this great new business opportunity I'm working with. Want to know more?"

And the cost to them to create this illusion, this total fabrication of wealth, these smoke and mirrors? A few hundred a month to lease a "poor man's Porsche." (You'll notice they weren't handing out 911s!)

If you've got someone telling you what you have to charge, who you can and can't sell to, what you have to say to them, the exact script you have to use, the exact marketing you have to use, and a fixed set of products that you have to sell – then you DON'T have a lifestyle business.

That's not even a business. That's a JOB. You have a JOB – one that you've paid a few hundred quid for, and one that pays you commission only. Slow hand clap.

Between the MLMers and the VC brigade, us lifestyle business owners have been given a bad name, quite undeservedly, I believe. To me, lifestyle doesn't mean small. It doesn't mean unambitious. Sure, you're not necessarily shooting for the moon. You're not going to, as Steve Jobs would say, "put a ding in the universe" with a lifestyle business, but you can put a hell of a dent in YOUR FAMILY'S universe. You can make a huge difference to a small number of people with a lifestyle business.

You've got a lot less risk, you're more likely to succeed, more flexible and able to react quickly to changing market conditions. You're going to have less debt, less stress, and you're likely to actually enjoy it more too! If you control the business, then you control the lifestyle.

How I created my own lifestyle business

The turning point for me came in 2009 when the first of my children arrived on the scene. Suddenly, the business I was building (aiming for 150 staff, £12 million turnover, skyscrapers, helicopters and yachts) wasn't the business I wanted. It wasn't the LIFESTYLE that I wanted. So I decided there and then, to turn it into a lifestyle business.

My business would exist purely to fund and allow the lifestyle I wanted – to be there for my children, to always be present whilst they're growing up, to show them the world, and to have the best possible relationship with them.

Then the voice in my head started up.

"That's not very ambitious, is it?"

But why not? Why couldn't I have a business that funded my lifestyle, but was also ambitious?

I didn't need to "be" a millionaire; I could "live like" a millionaire. I didn't need to own the country estate – I needed to have the spare time to enjoy someone else's (National Trust, or English Heritage). I didn't need to OWN a yacht and a supercar – I wanted to be able to hire them either for the day or lease them for longer if I want.

I didn't need to OWN a villa in Spain and an apartment in the South of France. If I'd got the assets to throw off excess cash, I could rent villas and apartments all over the world via sites like Airbnb or James Villas, without having to worry about the maintenance and upkeep of them.

 BIG IDEA...

You don't need to BE a millionaire to LIVE like a millionaire.

I didn't need to own ANYTHING. All I needed was time and cash flow. To achieve that didn't require a £12m turnover or 150 members of staff. I just needed a small team, who were looking to achieve great things, whilst sculpting the business around the lives that we all wanted. So I took out everyone's contracts, ripped them up, and re-wrote them to include the following paragraphs:

> "We are an 'Ambitious Lifestyle Business'. The ethos of the company is REALLY important. Everyone works from home. For most people there are NO fixed hours, however, there will be some core times which will need to be covered, and these will be discussed with you separately.

> If you need a day off TODAY, or a week off NEXT WEEK, as long as it's not going to cause the business to suffer or lose us customers, you'll get it. If you're not feeling at your best, I'd rather you did a few hours focused work and take a Duvet Day than sit at your desk clock-watching for eight hours feeling lousy and achieving nothing.

> That's the 'lifestyle' element of our ethos taken care of... now the 'ambition'... We carry NO passengers. Everyone WORKS from home. Everyone puts in a shift, and you're expected to work a full week most weeks.

> Because we're flexible over hours and time off generally, we'll also ask you to go 'above and beyond' whenever the business needs you to (usually when the shit hits the fan, or during peak sales periods).

> We're in business to make a profit, and whilst we're more than happy to 'give' in terms of flexibility, anyone who prefers to 'take, take take' and generally takes the piss doesn't stay with us long! There is no such thing as 'not my job' in this job!"

So, all of my team now know, and in fact, I'll tell anyone who'll listen – "We are an ambitious lifestyle business."

Of course, everyone wants the lifestyle, but we need to make sure that we don't lose sight of the fact that we are a business. There are bills to be paid, and we want to make money. We have ambition. We want to grow. We want to get bigger. Sure, we don't have moonshot ambitions.

We are not looking to change the world. We're not looking to completely disrupt an industry and take on the establishment. But then we're not emulating Steve Jobs, Elon Musk, Richard Branson. We're not studying these billionaires and saying "let's copy these people".

We are a lifestyle business first and foremost, so all of our team members work from home. Literally, every single person in the business – from the MD to the metaphorical tea lady, all work from home. They choose their own hours, within reason. Often there are certain things that need doing at certain times of the day, but if you're a coder who works better hunched over your laptop from nine at night till three in the morning, crack on. That's what you do. As long as the work gets done.

As long as the tasks get done, we are happy. That is the lifestyle.

If you want to be there to pick your Mum up from a doctor's appointment or have a driving lesson, or head to the gym, or you want to do the school runs. Crack on. Yeah. We're flexible. Go do that. If you're just feeling a bit under the weather, you want to have a day off, go do it, you know, but never forget that we're a business.

As I'm writing this chapter, the Cheltenham Festival is about to get underway. It's THE biggest event in the horse racing calendar, and as we own a sports betting company, it's our busiest time of the year. So NO-ONE can take this week (or any of the preceding three or four weeks) off.

The level of work ramps up significantly about two weeks before the festival starts, and for the duration of the festival (which is only four days), most of my team work from the minute they wake up until the minute they go to bed.

In other words – it's payback time! When the shit hits the fan (server crashes) or at certain other periods of the year (big sales campaigns and major sporting events), we're slave drivers, and the team have to contend with spinning 30 different plates at the same time, whilst working 14+ hour days, weekends, you name it – because we're an ambitious business.

And then when the pressure's off, we go back to our default – an "ambitious LIFESTYLE business" – often the team will book holidays and time off just after a major campaign, and we survive with skeleton staff for this period, as I appreciate how important it is for them to recharge their batteries, and come back refreshed, revitalised, and still in love with their job.

So, back to the question I asked you at the start of this chapter – What lifestyle do YOU want your business to provide you with?

Whatever it is that you want, I implore you:

Be AMBITIOUS.

Remember it's all about the LIFESTYLE.

And don't forget that you're running a BUSINESS, not a charity.

Ambitious. Lifestyle. Business.

FIVE MAGIC INGREDIENTS...

"George didn't say a word. He felt quite trembly. He knew something tremendous had taken place that morning. For a few brief moments he had touched with the very tips of his fingers the edge of a magic world."

Roald Dahl
George's Marvellous Medicine

I've split the ideas and topics in this book into roughly five sections – these cover the "magic ingredients" that, for me, are the building blocks of any success. If you study anyone who's ever achieved anything of note and reverse engineer exactly HOW they did it – it's likely that they'll have ticked off at least three or four of these magic ingredients.

You don't need all five to be successful, and many people have become successful having only achieved one or two of them, but if you want to give yourself a better chance of success (whatever success looks like for you – whether that's making more money, better health, improved relationships, passing exams, learning to drive, selling a business, or raising children), you can use these magic ingredients to design HOW you're going to succeed – and to give yourself an infinitely better chance of actually achieving it.

But first, would you like to know a secret?

Every single one of these "magic ingredients" actually contains no "magic" at all – they're just routines, habits and characteristics that your average, every-day, bog-standard human can use to APPEAR super-human. And they're the building blocks on which I've built my businesses over the last two decades.

They've made such an impact for me, that I've even gone to the trouble of painting them on the wall in my office, in foot-high capital letters, so that I see them, and can live by them on a daily basis. (If you've watched any of my videos before, you've no-doubt seen them before! If not, look out for the photographic evidence later in the book...)

Literally, every single piece of success I've had, I can usually point to three or four of the magic ingredients being in place. On the rare occasions that I score five out of five – well, that's where the magic happens.

So, are you ready to hear about magic ingredient number one?

Magic ingredient #1 – GOALS

We'll deep-dive into the stunning turquoise waters of goals in the next chapter, but it's safe to say that most people who've ever read a personal development book, watched a documentary, or listened to a podcast will have heard about the importance of goal setting. If you've been listening to any of my podcasts or watched any of my videos, you'll have heard me banging on about them – a LOT.

Without a goal, how do you know where you're heading? What you're aiming for? What the destination is? And if you don't know the destination, how do you know if you're on course? If a 747 sits on the runway at Heathrow Airport and wants to fly to JFK Airport in New York, the pilots will put together a flight plan, plotting the exact route they're going to take. They don't just take off, turn left and hope for the best. Then they spend the next eight hours constantly re-calculating their trajectory, to make sure they stay on the plan.

That's what you need to do with your goals. Otherwise, who knows where on earth you might end up...

> Alice: "Would you tell me, please, which way I ought to go from here?"
>
> The Cheshire Cat: "That depends a good deal on where you want to get to."
>
> Alice: "I don't much care where."
>
> The Cheshire Cat: "Then it doesn't matter which way you go."
>
> Alice: "So long as I get somewhere."
>
> The Cheshire Cat: "Oh, you're sure to do that, if only you walk long enough."
>
> Lewis Carroll
> Alice in Wonderland

Magic ingredient #2 – DESIRE

What's the difference between "Can't" and "Don't want to"?

It's your desire.

Too many people say they "can't" do things, that they're actually perfectly capable of, but just don't want to do. They don't have sufficient desire to do it, so they shut their brain down by saying "I can't do that".

I've never used the cliché "There's no such word as can't" on my children, mainly because there IS such a word as can't. (You will find it in the official Oxford English Dictionary.) I prefer to ask them to clarify what they mean.

Do you mean you're not capable of doing it?

Because if so, you meant to say "I can't do it YET." Keep on trying.

Or did you mean you don't WANT to do it?

Because, unless it is physically impossible, the thing that you "can't do" HAS to be something you either can't do YET or something you don't WANT to do. If it's the former, more practice, more training, more perseverance will get you there. If it's the latter, then you have a problem – a lack of desire.

Most people fail to achieve their goals because they don't DESIRE them enough to do the nasty stuff that's needed to get the job done. If my goal is a washboard stomach, with rock-hard abs, and fantastic definition, then I've got to REALLY desire that goal in order to resist all the temptations that will come my way over the prolonged period of time that those abs are going to develop.

Which do I desire more? Abs or Cake? Ben & Jerry's or sit-ups? Steamed broccoli or chocolate brownie?

Mmmm, brownie...

> *"When you want to succeed as bad as you want to breathe, then you'll be successful."*
>
> *Eric Thomas*

Magic ingredient #3 – KNOWLEDGE

Knowledge is one of the easiest of the magic ingredients to collect. It's literally all around you. Pretty much every major city in the world has at least one library, where you can go for free, and read books – books that have been written by people who have already done what it is that you want to do. They've taken the time to document the blueprint for your success, and you can have it – for free!

You've got a book in your hands right now, so I know I'm preaching to the converted here, and I won't patronise you too much by harping on about the importance of learning (I'll save that for a later chapter!), but it's worth remembering just how much knowledge is out there for you to tap into – whether that's audiobooks, documentaries, podcasts, white papers, YouTube videos, online courses, offline courses, and of course traditional books like this one.

I dare say you're carrying a mobile phone around with you now, which, most likely, will have access to the internet . That means that you're carrying around the entire collection of all human knowledge – since the dawn of time, in your pocket, all day, every day.

And to think my teachers used to utter that famous line to get us to stop using calculators and do mental arithmetic – "What are you going to do when you leave school, carry a calculator with you everywhere you go?" – erm, yep!

And a telephone.

And a television.

And a radio.

And a diary.

And a camera.

And a dictionary.

And a world atlas.

And the entire works of Shakespeare. And an encyclopaedia (that's updated every minute of every day).

How do you think I went from being a civil servant, who knew nothing about the internet , or marketing, to someone who owned an internet marketing company?

Knowledge.

I was like a sponge those first few years – teaching myself everything I needed to know in order to have a successful business, in an area that I'd previously known precisely nothing about – whether it was "Rich Dad, Poor Dad" or "Internet Marketing for Dummies", if I wasn't working the day job, or I wasn't working in the business, I had a book in my hands.

The more I learned, the more I earned.

And that's still true today – the more I learn, the more I earn.

"The worst thing you can ever do is think that you know enough. Never stop learning. Ever. I've always treated the world as my classroom, soaking up lessons and stories to fuel my path forward."

Arnold Schwarzenegger

Magic ingredient #4 – ENVIRONMENT

Not to be confused with Greenpeace, melting icecaps or global warming – this is the environment that you surround yourself with. The people you hang around with, what you choose to watch and listen to, how you spend your spare time.

I'm sure you've heard the saying that "you are the sum of the five people you spend the most time with" – this is one of those clichés that gets thrown out regularly, usually by someone who wants you to hang around with THEM, but there's actually a really powerful truth in this cliché.

As you'll read in a later chapter, when I was younger I used to hang around with a bunch of arseholes, and what do you know... it turned me into an arsehole. Nowadays, I hang around with ambitious lifestyle business owners, entrepreneurs, millionaires, and even the occasional billionaire – and it's made me a better person.

I don't watch the soaps, X-Factor, or celebrity paint-drying (I hardly watch any TV in fact) – I've replaced inane TV junk with documentaries and YouTube videos,

I've replaced listening to the radio with listening to audiobooks and podcasts, and I've replaced drunken chats with Dodgy Dave at the pub, with quality networking with successful people.

If you want to lose weight, but your cupboards are full of biscuits and cake, your fridge is full of chocolate, your freezer's full of ice cream and your friends like nothing better than to pig out on takeaways, then you're going to find it tough.

But fill your cupboards with nuts and seeds, your fridge with fresh fruit and veg, your freezer with frozen berries and smoothie ingredients, and hang around with gym buddies, or join a running club – and things get a little bit easier.

This stuff works like osmosis. It just can't help but rub off on you.

You literally do become a product of your environment.

Junk in, junk out.

Success in, success out.

> *"If you want to soar like an eagle in life, you can't be flocking with the turkeys."*
>
> *Warren Buffett*

Magic ingredient #5 – ACTION!

There's an old saying isn't there – "Nothing happens in business until someone sells something", and so it is with the fifth, and last, of our magic ingredients.

This is THE vital ingredient.

You can line all the other four up perfectly – You can have a GOAL that's perfectly aligned to your DESIRE, you can get all the KNOWLEDGE you need to prosper, and set up your ENVIRONMENT to give you the best chance of success – but if you don't take any ACTION, you'll achieve the square root of bugger all.

I mentioned earlier that I've got these five magic ingredients painted on the wall in my office. What I didn't tell you is that the first four are about a foot high, painted in charcoal grey. But Magic Ingredient #5 – ACTION! is a little bit bigger, in bright red, with an exclamation mark next to it. I want a constant reminder that, although there's no such thing as a silver bullet when it comes to success, taking regular ACTION (on the right things) is the next best thing to it.

What you know doesn't matter, it's what you DO that counts.

Take "I want to fit in the 30-inch jeans by the time I go on holiday" as the goal.

Once you're absolutely sure that you DESIRE it badly enough to put up with the pain of doing what's necessary, you've got the blueprint for how you're going to get there (KNOWLEDGE), and you've adjusted your ENVIRONMENT accordingly – you've bought the lycra and the running shoes, and your fridge is full of fruit and veg, what happens then?

Do you automatically slide into those jeans on the morning of your holiday? Of course you bloody don't.

You've got to actually WEAR the lycra. You've got to actually RUN in the running shoes. You've got to actually EAT the fruit and veg. You've got to do more activity at the gym than just taking selfies and making playlists. It's no good just hiring a personal trainer and a nutritionist. You've got to actually turn up to your sessions with them, and then DO what they tell you to.

This is where most people go wrong – they spend most of their time in the planning stages of their goals, because, let's face it – that's the fun part – the bit where you get to imagine how amazing your life is going to be when you've achieved your goal.

You can create all sorts of fancy planners, to-do lists, all colour coded with neat labels and stickers on them. You can do just a bit more research.

But sooner or later you've got to actually get off your arse and DO SOMETHING.

Take some ACTION.

You know what you're going to ACHIEVE by doing it (#1 – GOALS).

You know WHY you need to do it (#2 – DESIRE).

You know WHAT you need to do (#3 – KNOWLEDGE)

Everything is in place to HELP you do it (#4 – ENVIRONMENT).

All that remains is for YOU to actually DO it.

One step... at a time... One foot... in front... of the other.

Take ACTION.

BIG IDEA...

The five magic ingredients:
- Goals
- Desire
- Knowledge
- Environment
- Action

"If more information was the answer, then we'd all be Billionaires with perfect abs."

Derek Sivers

MAGIC INGREDIENT #1 – GOALS
(A.K.A. CHANGE YOUR WAYS IN 90 DAYS...)

*"You have brains in your head, and feet in your shoes.
You can steer yourself any direction you choose."*

Dr. Seuss

I'm sat here writing this in the middle of January. I've just returned from the gym, where – yep, you've guessed it, there wasn't a space in the car park, the changing rooms were stacked with people trying to squeeze into the new lycra gear they bought last week, and the swimming pool resembled the shipping lanes of the English Channel.

It was of course, full of "New Year, New Me" types, who will be conspicuous by their absence come the second week of February. By Valentine's Day, our local gym looks more like the opening scenes from '28 Days Later'.

It's fair to say, therefore, that for most people, new year resolutions just don't work. The only exception I can think of to this rule is the machine that is Arnold Schwarzenegger, who would write down his goals on New Year's Eve every year. And no piddly little "I will try and lose weight" or "I will try to drink less this year" for Arnold.

No, his "resolutions" were more along the lines of:

"I will learn English"
"I will move to America"
"I will win Mr Olympia"
"I will win Mr Universe"
"I will make a million dollars in real estate"
"I will create a mail order business"
"I will get the leading role in a Hollywood movie"
"I will do a comedy movie when no-one thinks I can do comedy"
*"I will be elected Governor of the State of California –
the highest political office I can legally hold"*
"I will write a New York Times bestselling book"

And of course, he's achieved every single one of those.

His "resolutions" now are even loftier – to literally change the world by championing real action around climate change.

For me though, Arnie doesn't set resolutions, he sets goals. Big-arsed, scary goals that kept him awake at night. Goals that he probably didn't know how to achieve in the beginning. But he did something that made it much, much more likely that he would achieve them – he wrote them down. He found out what he needed to do to achieve them. And he did it. Simple as that.

For us mere mortals though, it's probably not quite that simple. It's easy to sit there as the clock strikes midnight and another year rolls around to say "I'm going to lose 20 pounds this year", but after about two weeks of hitting the gym and living on grilled chicken and steamed broccoli, to see that you're only a whopping two and a half pounds lighter, you're going to feel like giving up.

Willpower is not limitless

And that's because you've been relying on willpower alone – I think of willpower like an iPhone's battery – it doesn't last long, and if you want to actually achieve anything over a sustained period of time, you're gonna need to top it up! In order to replenish your willpower battery, the best place to look is at another of our magic ingredients – DESIRE. What kept Arnold putting in six hours a day at the gym, eating nothing (and I mean nothing!) outside of his meal plan, doing the daily habits of training right, eating right, training harder and harder? It was his desire to beat his competitors. For some people, it's fear of failure. But for Arnold, he wanted to prove that he was better than ANYONE else – and he had a REALLY strong desire to prove it, in front of massive audiences on TV.

If you don't have a REALLY strong, burning desire to achieve your goals, then you're going to find it really hard – UNLESS...

You can find a way to change your daily habits and routines. That's what drives real change. And can help you achieve your goals.

If you've ever worked in an office, or anywhere remotely corporate, you'll no doubt have heard of SMART goals. Well, I hate acronyms, as I can never remember what they stand for (apart from "Never Eat

Shredded Wheat" to figure out how to read a compass), and SMART goals are a load of rubbish anyway.

I think the "R" stands for "realistic" – but who wants to be realistic? If I'd only ever done what was "realistic", what I was qualified to do, I'd be sweeping the streets somewhere. I certainly wouldn't have launched an internet marketing business despite knowing nothing about either the internet or marketing, let alone be mentoring ambitious lifestyle business owners, presenting a podcast and writing books about it. That's just not realistic.

I've just googled SMART goals to see what they do actually stand for – turns out that "what do smart goals stand for" is one of the most frequently-searched terms for SMART goals, so I'm clearly not the only one who can't remember what the bloody hell it's supposed to remind you of.

SMART goals are – Specific, Measurable, Achievable, Realistic, and Timely. Bet you don't remember them all a week from today. I know I won't. And isn't "achievable" the same as "realistic"? "Specific" and "Measurable" are pretty damn similar too now that I come to think of it.

I think your goals need to tick just TWO boxes – you have to know EXACTLY WHAT you want to achieve, and EXACTLY WHEN you want to achieve it. So no more "I want to lose weight" – it's now "I want to fit into those 30inch jeans, by the time I go on holiday". Instead of "I'm going to work harder at school", turn it into "I'm going to average a B-grade by the end of the spring term"

Rather than having a vague, long-term goal like "I want to lose weight this year", I prefer to have specific, 90-day goals. Literally, every three months, I'm sitting down and setting out my goals for the next quarter. It's a short enough timescale not to be overwhelming, but a long enough period to actually make a difference. Most people overestimate what they can achieve in the short term, and underestimate what's possible in the long term, so I feel 90 days strikes just the right balance.

The power of 90-day plans

Ninety days is long enough to achieve something pretty significant. You're not going to change the world in three months, but you can make some pretty huge lifestyle changes – and after three months, those are going to become habits – things that you do without even thinking about it.

If the desire was high enough (a gun to your child's head for example), most people would be capable of doubling their business in a year. But setting that as a goal? "Impossible" would be most people's reply. How about "increase your business by just 19%" in the next three months? Do that EVERY three months, and after a year, guess what – you've doubled your business!

Try and get some real clarity on your goals. How much is the deposit for that Disney holiday? When would the balance be due? How much is a gardener? How many hours per month would you need? What's the exact model, spec and colour of your dream car? And how much are the monthly payments? How many new customers does that equate to? Am I willing to do what's necessary to achieve these goals – in other words, are these actual goals, or just dreams?

 BIG IDEA...

Are you setting GOALS or just dreams?

Once again, DESIRE holds the key – ask yourself not just "What do I want?" but rather "Why do I want this? What difference will it make to my life, and the lives of those I care about? What will happen to them if I don't achieve it?" – because that's what's going to keep you going when the willpower runs out.

What happens when your car skids out of control, and all you can focus on is "don't hit the lamppost", "don't hit the lamppost"?

Yep, nine times out of ten you hit the damn lamppost because you get what you focus on. It's the same with your goals – aim to "stop losing customers" and you'll lose customers. Aim your energy instead towards "retaining customers", and your brain will set to work finding ways to do just that – you can't ask your brain to go and find ways NOT to do something. Try it if you like. Ask your brain not to think of the famous McDonalds arches. How did that go? Fancy a Big Mac yet?

Ask for what you DO want, not what you don't want.

That applies not only to short-term goals but the "North Star" long term biggies too. Goals that are more of an over-arching destination that you're heading towards – a "North Star". If sailors ever get lost at sea, they can always find their way back on course by finding the North Star in the night sky – and if you've got real clarity and focus on where your long-term strategy is taking you, then your North Star can guide you too.

BIG IDEA...

You get what you FOCUS on.

The 90-day goals are the tactics that are going to get me there. They keep me moving in the right direction towards those annual goals. I set three goals per 90 days. They're pretty big goals. Nothing that I could achieve in a few days. They all require pretty big effort, lots of moving parts come together, but they are big things that will move my business or my life forward.

What I then do is I break down those three goals further, into monthly goals. That's three goals for 90 days, and three goals every month. That basically will help me achieve the overarching goal.

As an example, my big three goals for the next 90 days are to:

1.   Launch a podcast

2.   Write this book

3.   Relaunch a website

Those are three pretty major things. They're not the sort of things that I could achieve in a weekend or a few days just by putting in a few hours here and there. That requires some pretty hefty work.

Putting a plan together

I can break those goals down and say, "Okay, what do I do in month one?"

Month one, I start recording the podcast. I'll also get the audio transcribed from the podcasts that I'm going to use in the book, so I've started writing the book. Then we'll also put together a step by step list of everything that needs to happen to relaunch the website.

That's month one's goals – three actionable items that I can take that get me closer to my three 90-day goals, which will then keep me on track for my overall annual goals.

Month two, I will launch the podcast. Get it on iTunes etc., start promoting it. I'll turn the first six chapters of the book from draft version (which I got transcribed last month) into finished chapters, and have this month's podcast episodes transcribed for the same purpose. I'll then get the design and structure of the website relaunch ready to go.

We're now two months in, and every step I take gets me closer to nailing those three big 90-day goals.

Month three, and it's full-on marketing campaigns for the podcast, 12 chapters of the book are finished, with another four in draft. The book's going to take longer than 90 days, but the 90-day plan gives me the momentum that means I'll be at least halfway there with more than 30,000 words written, ready to send to an editor. I've also then got a full plan to market and relaunch the website, which I can deploy in my next 90-day period.

Ninety days in, and I've achieved a hell of a lot.

The 90-day planner is my satnav – I refer to it all the time to make sure I'm on track. When I'm planning out my week, and want to know what to fill my time with, I just glance at my 90-day plan and say "Right, it's month one. I need to start recording podcasts, so let's block out 11am until 1pm on Monday to record and upload an episode. On Wednesday morning, I'll have the transcription back from that podcast, so let's block out a few hours to convert the draft into a finished chapter. On Thursday, I'm blocking out the whole day to meet with the designer for the website relaunch.

 BIG IDEA...

Block out time for the important stuff, and PROTECT that time with your life.

I protect that time like it's gold-dust. Nothing, and I mean nothing, gets in the way of my 90-day goals. I can then fill all the other "stuff" that happens in every business around the important tasks that keep me moving forwards. And every day, I'm doing something that moves me towards my goals.

My daily tasks keep me on track for my weekly goal. My weekly goal helps me achieve the monthly goal, which enables me to hit the 90-day goals. And if I hit all three of my 90-day goals, every 90 days, then over the course of a year, I achieve 12 HUGE things that really propel my business forward – the stuff that really makes a difference to the bottom line, and the quality of my family members' lives.

Planning on steroids

There are many ways that you can make your goal setting more effective:

1. Link your goals to your desires. Don't rely on willpower alone.

2. Make them specific. And time-based. Not "I will lose weight", but "I will be 13st 7lb or less on May 17th".

3. Write them down. That's what Arnie did. And if it's good enough for the Terminator, it's good enough for me.

4. Share them – tell someone, anyone who'll listen. Sharing a goal publicly makes you more accountable to it, and more likely to stick at it.

If you tell me that you want to lose 20 pounds, and I happen to see you pigging out on a bucket meal at KFC, you're going to get a little bit of a ribbing there, and knowing that others are "looking out for you" can help keep you on track.

My personal preference though is to set goals that are linked to really strong desires, write them down in my 90-day planner, and share them publicly with as many people as possible (hosting a podcast is a good way to do this!) – then add consequences...

You can use public shaming ("If I don't lose 20 pounds by March 31st, I'll run down the street naked"), a betting pool ("We'll all put £100 in the pot, and whoever loses the most body fat wins the lot"), or the big stick of the anti-charity. I've done this before with some private coaching clients where I've got them to write out a pretty big cheque (up to you what's big – I've used £500 and £1,000 in the past) to someone they HATE – someone they would do anything to avoid giving money to – and I sit on that cheque for them.

If they hit their goal, we have a party and rip up the cheque.

If they don't hit their goal, I mail the cheque.

Human beings are wired up to do MORE to avoid pain than we will do to get pleasure. So whilst dropping a couple of jean sizes, looking and feeling fantastic would be great, you're more likely to stick to the salads and gym sessions if you know it's going to cost you a few hundred quid if you don't – especially if that money's going to someone who you wouldn't spit on if they were on fire!

 BIG IDEA...

There should be CONSEQUENCES for not hitting your goals.

Some "popular" anti-charities include:

- KKK
- American Nazi Party
- Donald Trump Election Fund
- Margaret Thatcher Legacy Fund
- Manchester United Fan Club
- Liverpool Fan Club
- Your competitors

If you want someone independent to do this for you, have a look at www.stickk.com. They'll hold your funds in ESCROW, and verify whether you have achieved your goal or not before either giving your money back or releasing it to your anti-charity.

Pinning your hopes on a collage

A good way to help visualise your goals, and put your subconscious brain to work on achieving them is to use vision boards – before you think I've gone all woo-woo and new age on you, I'm NOT telling you to "ask the universe" for anything here, nor am I preaching any of the "if you wish for it hard enough, it'll happen" BS that only happens in Disney movies. I'm talking about a scientific process, that athletes have been using for decades. Olympic weightlifters who VISUALISED lifting weights (i.e. did no actual training!) saw similar brain patterns and muscle gains as those who did a normal workout. The brain was "tricked" into thinking it was doing something it wasn't – it isn't able to distinguish between visualisation and reality.

I too scoffed at this at first – I remember thinking that there's no way putting a picture of a Porsche 911 and a house in the country on a vision board is going to suddenly make those items materialise out of thin air. And I was right – but then my DESIRE (magic ingredient #2) for those items was actually quite low – I wasn't willing to pay the price to get them.

So I re-jigged my vision board, this time adding things that I really DID want to achieve in the next twelve months – there was a new car on there, but it was a Toyota GT86, not a 911. I don't want to move to a big house in the country, but I do want to add an extension to my home, adding a dining room, balcony, bigger bedrooms, walk-in wardrobe and a sauna.

The sauna was an interesting example, as the image I found online, that I pasted onto my vision board was of a really cool, large sauna, with loads of floor-to-ceiling glass, chrome fittings and large matte black tiles on the floor and walls. I didn't have space in the remodelled home for that spec, so I ended up with a much more traditional wooden look, with real stone tiles on the floor. Beggars can't be choosers, eh?

Also on the board were images of holidays to Tenerife, and Walt Disney World in Florida, along with a swimming pool (which I also wanted to fit into the house remodel), a Monopoly board (I was looking to do my first property investment that year), a movie poster from the film "Date Night" (I wanted to take half-days on a Friday to spend with my wife, and the kids after school), a picture of a gardener (I wanted to hire one), a cleaner (ditto!), and pictures of bands that I wanted to see that year (Catfish and the Bottlemen, Noel Gallagher, Biffy Clyro, and Arctic Monkeys).

Whilst your business may well fund your lifestyle, I firmly believe that your vision board should contain at least 75% life goals and only around 25% business goals. It's the fun, the excitement, the desire to live a better life that will keep you on track to actually achieve the business goals. Setting the level of "fun" you want to have in a year also forces you to take some time out to reward yourself, to step off that hamster wheel once in a while and pat yourself on the back for the awesome work that you do.

I also added some pictures to remind me where I wanted to take my business and investments strategy over the year – pictures of foreign exchange boards (focus on Forex trading), silver bullion (buy loads of it!), and some custom images to remind me to focus on "conversion rate optimisation", with the ultimate goal of doubling the annual profit dividend payable to Jason and me.

Finally, there was a photo of me, taken at an affiliate conference in 2007, where I was part of a panel of "experts" (I use the term loosely!), giving a 60 minute Q&A session to around 150 people. I'd really enjoyed helping people out over the years, and wanted to focus more on mentoring and helping out newbies in business over the coming year.

I created this collage of 15 or so images using a free online collage creator, and set it as my desktop background and lock screen wallpaper on my computer – this meant that these images on my "vision board" were the first thing I saw before I started work every single time I sat down at my desk to work. Sometimes I'd look at the image for a minute or two, ticking off those I had achieved, and working through how I was going to achieve the others, but on the whole, I just got on with my work. Over the course of one year, I probably saw that image for two or three seconds at a time, something like 1,500 times. Talk about subliminal brain-washing.

Towards the end of the year, I started work on my vision board for the following 12 months, and took stock of what I had achieved from that very first set of images – and I was astounded: Out of the 15 items on there, I'd ticked off 12 of them!

(Arctic Monkeys didn't tour that year, and we literally couldn't fit the swimming pool into the remodelled house, so technically I only failed to complete ONE of the goals that I could have achieved!)

I also spotted something else that was really interesting (which is where I WILL go all "law of attraction" on you) – I might not have been able to fit a swimming pool into the extension, but that year I did join a local swimming club and was swimming three times a week. And in place of the swimming pool in the house remodel, we added a large en suite bathroom.

Sarah and I went shopping for the fittings, shower cubicle, tiles etc. for this bathroom one day, ordered what we liked, and a few months later the builders finally moved out and we were able to start using this fantastic new en suite.

It was an en suite that was far bigger than it needed to be, with loads of chrome fittings, matte black tiles on the wall and floor, and the pièce de résistance – a huge sheet of floor-to-ceiling glass for the shower.

It wasn't until I went to take down my vision board that I noticed it – the picture of the sauna that I WANTED – the one we couldn't fit in, which meant I ended up with a traditional wooden one. We'd only gone and recreated it in our new en suite, almost EXACTLY to the same detail as that cool sauna I had wanted – everything from the tiles, to the chrome, to the towel rails, to the floor-to-ceiling glass, it was all there. That goes to show what the power of the sub-conscious mind can achieve given just 12 short months.

Could you make bigger plans?

I'm actually starting to think even longer term now, setting 20-year plans for some of our businesses, but even those still have the 90-day plan to keep us on track – the 20-year plan is the North Star destination. You may want to go to the moon, but you've got to build the rocket first, and learn how to fly it!

You need to be careful how high you set your goals – there's no point setting goals that you KNOW you're going to achieve, just so you can "tick them off" – you've got to push yourself (and if you can't push yourself, get your arse into our Facebook group – www.bigidea.co.uk/facebook – and WE'LL bloody well push you), but also you need to set goals that are just outside of your grasp right now, without appearing totally unachievable – otherwise your motivation will disappear right along with your willpower.

Don't let that stop you asking stupid questions though, as you never know where the answer might take you. One of our private clients is a tennis coach, and he was telling us all about his five-year plan one day. I asked him "what would need to happen to achieve that five-year goal in nine months?"

He was totally taken aback, he'd never thought about it before – he just thought "well, if I keep on doing what I do now, it'll take me five years" – it was only someone planting the "could it be done quicker?" question in his head that got him thinking along the lines of "well, I could hire a developer, and launch here, then work on X, Y and Z myself before doing a PR campaign, etc., etc."

From there, we were able to reverse-engineer the business he wanted and achieve five years' worth of growth in three 90-day periods. What needs to happen in YOUR business in the next 90 days to achieve your hopes and dreams?

I'D LIKE TO OWN A REAL BUSINESS ONE DAY...

"Most people overestimate what they can achieve in one year, and underestimate what they can achieve in ten"

Bill Gates

Around nine months into my "business career", I was interviewed by my local newspaper, the Plymouth Evening Herald.

Even though the internet had been around in some form or another for almost ten years by this point, "man has website" was still deemed to be newsworthy in Plymouth in 2001, so in response to my "press release" (I sent them a letter saying something along the lines of "I live in Plymouth and have a website. Would you like to write about me?"), the Herald dispatched a photographer to take my mugshot, and I spent ten minutes or so chatting to a junior reporter, who probably drew the short straw, or was being punished in some way by having to cover this mundane story.

An insight into the goals I set in 2001

Of course, at the time, this was HUGE for me – I was still working the day job, but now I was actually FAMOUS too – check me out on page 34 of the business pull-out, just before the classified ads. I bought copies for all my friends and family, framed a pristine version for my wall, and waited for the phone to ring. Surely it was only a matter of time now before the national press picked up on the story of this hot new whizz kid, who was surely destined to become the next twenty-something dotcom millionaire?

Unfortunately, Fleet Street must have missed the memo, as the phone didn't ring. At all. I had no further coverage, local or national – and that article gave me no new customers (turns out "man has access to the internet " would have been newsworthy in Plymouth in 2001!) – but the article did remain framed on my wall for a few years, until we

Business Herald ■ April 2001

Evening Herald, Tuesd

Website Inexperience is no barrier for net entrepreneur

Freebies pave way for John

e business

NINE months ago John Lamerton had never had access to the internet.

He now runs a popular site advertising freegoods over the internet and is planning to launch three more sites in June, all part-time from his home in Chaddlewood.

John has managed to launch his successful site with no formal training or internet experience, picking up tips along the way to improve it and put him in the position to think about expansion.

He said: "I am a civil servant by day, and have been for six years now.

"Last autumn I got on to the internet for the first time and saw a huge potential.

"I decided to build my own site, no experience, no training and I got it up there.

"It was terrible.

"But there are plenty of people using the internet who will offer advice and help, so I took their advice and have just relaunched the site at 2001freebies.co.uk

"It now has about 500 links to all kinds of things people can get for free, with a few clicks of the mouse."

Opportunity

The site links to all kinds of offers of...

People love freebies, you can't lose really.

The three new sites will include another set of freebies, one for prizes and one for bargains.

John said: "There is a lot of opportunity out there and you don't really need a lot of experience and training to get started.

"In recent months, internet businesses have not been doing too well, but I am not making the mistake of spending huge amounts of money on advertising.

"Instead I am building up the sites and allow things to spread by word of mouth.

"The plan is to build it up to a fully-fledged business but I am in no rush.

"I just want to do it properly, take advantage of the opportunities and try not to make too many mistakes along the way."

John creates his web pages using the PageBuilder package.

ALL FREE: John Lamerton, with some of the freebies promoted through his website

Picture Lucy Davies EH-79420

Credit: Lucy Davies, Plymouth Herald

moved house, at which point it took up residence in the place where all the crap you don't know what to do with (but don't want to throw out) goes – the garage.

And that's where it stayed – until last year when we had a bit of a ruthless tidy-up, and I came across this old Herald article once again, now 16 years old, with a 22-year-old version of me (carrying a load of extra weight and with far too much hair gel) grinning out at me. I didn't realise it at the time, but that article was going to serve a BIG purpose – it was going to document just how low I was setting my ambitions at the time, in comparison to what I'd actually achieved over those 16 years.

You can see why – the opening line was "Nine months ago John Lamerton had never had access to the internet " (I told you internet access was newsworthy back then!), so I could hardly have predicted that I would go on to forge a career out of this internet business that I still knew hardly anything about, earn several million pounds, and go on to write a book about the whole shebang.

But I could have at least set my sights a LITTLE higher. In the end, I settled for the following about my long term ambitions for the business:

The plan is to build it up into a fully-fledged business, but I'm in no rush. I'm not making the mistake of spending huge amounts of money on advertising. I'm allowing things to spread by word of mouth. I just want to try not to make too many mistakes along the way.

What happens when you let a civil servant set goals?

Present-day me would have had a field day with this quote. My (2001-me!) lack of confidence in my own abilities shines through like a beacon from that quote – I mean what sort of ambition is "I'd like to own a real business one day"? I had a "real business" right then – it just wasn't earning enough for me to leave the day job.

You can see the civil servant in me there too – totally focused on not making mistakes at any cost – even "mistakes" like "spending money on advertising" – I'm sure if I could go back to 2001 and tell myself that just three or four years later, I'd be spending more in a month on advertising than I used to earn in a year at the day job, 2001-me would have had a heart attack!

And don't get me started on "word of mouth" being my primary source of new customers. That's pretty much my number one pet hate now when I'm mentoring new clients, and they proudly announce that "word of mouth" is their biggest marketing channel. What they mean of course (and what I meant back in 2001) is that it's their only marketing channel.

BIG IDEA...

"Word of mouth" is NOT a marketing channel.

When I hear a new mentoring client say "word of mouth", they may actually be saying "word of mouth", but what I'm hearing is "I don't do ANYTHING to influence whether I get any new customers or not."

The danger of not thinking BIG

Now you may think I'm being a bit harsh on newbies (including 2001-me) in this chapter – after all, you don't know what you don't know. But take it from me, if I could have somehow got 2001-me to read this chapter, rather than spending those first few years "avoiding mistakes" and "allowing things to spread by word of mouth", I could have got some real momentum going from the very start.

We'll delve into the power of compounding with my business hero Warren Buffett in a later chapter, but for now just imagine what a difference it could have made to my current wealth if only I'd done things better in those first few years – "word of mouth" and "not spending money on advertising" for those first two years probably knocks a sizable six-figure sum off my current net worth after compounding,, and by the time I hit 60, that would have grown to a seven-figure loss.

Not thinking big enough = a BIG mistake.

 BIG IDEA...

Stop aiming so low. Think BIGGER.

That line I gave in the interview about being "in no rush" – that was total BS. I hated the day job. Absolutely HATED it. I wanted out of there as soon as humanly possible – and the internet business was my best shot at doing that.

What I should have said was something like "I'm going to leave my job and focus on my business full time as soon as it can afford to support me and my family. I'm going to try lots of new things, some of which will work, and some of which won't. I'm going to get myself a mentor so they can help me discern which is which."

Don't get me wrong – I'm very happy with where I am right now, and probably wouldn't change a thing given the chance to do it all again – but given this snapshot of my thinking 16 years ago, I'm reminded of the quote from Bill Gates that I opened this chapter with.

A year after that interview, I had indeed turned it into a "real business", but ten years later, I had no concept whatsoever of just how big it could have grown.

I'd underestimated what I could achieve in a year, and failed to conceive that I could achieve even 1% of what I eventually did, given a decade.

Having read this article again, I've recently adjusted my twenty-year business plans to take into account compounding some exceptional growth years – never again will I make the mistake of thinking small over the long term.

What could be worse than setting what (at the time) seem like stupidly-out-of-reach goals and just failing to hit them?

Setting what (in hindsight) are stupidly-safe goals, and just hitting them, that's what.

I BLAME RICHARD BRANSON...

"To do two things at once is to do neither."

Publilius Syrus

"It's the economy, stupid."

Bill Clinton was sat in his "war room" in 1991, working with his campaign team, brainstorming ways to unsettle the incumbent President of the United States of America, George Bush in the forthcoming 1992 election. By the time they'd finished, they had more than 30 different areas from which they could attack President Bush, from his handling of the invasion of Iraq, to health care, taxes, the environment, food and oil prices, and his relationship with the NRA.

But they also recognised that they wouldn't inflict the maximum damage on President Bush by attacking him on 30 different fronts – they didn't have the time or the budget to inflict death by a thousand paper cuts. It was then that James Carville, Clinton's lead strategist stepped forward, cleared the whiteboard completely, and wrote the following four words:

"It's the economy, stupid."

What did Bill Clinton stand for? The economy. What was his campaign all about? The economy. What was his job to turn EVERY conversation towards? It's the economy, stupid.

Clinton was given ONE task. ONE job. ONE message.

As the polls moved in Clinton's favour, Carville added another four words to the whiteboard "Don't forget health care" – ONE more thing to focus on.

Clinton, of course, won the 1992 election (and was re-elected in 1996 with ONE more message – I'm building a bridge to the 21st century.)

The sub-headline of this book is "simple, practical, tools and tactics to help your small business GROW" – and I make no apologies for this chapter being the simplest of them all. It's a tactic, a strategy, a way of life even, so unbelievably simple and straightforward that it would be very easy to dismiss it as obvious.

But just as "how to lose weight" is simple and obvious (eat less, exercise more), it would appear that putting the obvious, and the simple into practice on a daily basis is where many of us fall down – and as someone who used to carry around an extra five stone (that's about 70 pounds for our American friends) of blubber with me, and who used to work 100+ hour weeks whilst struggling to keep my head above water, I include myself in that sweeping generalisation.

Google gave me a kick in the balls

Jump in the DeLorean with me, and let's set the clock for early 2012.

I was running something like 10 or 12 different businesses – selling everything from private villa rentals to mobile phone insurance, live football streaming to car breakdown cover, online bingo to affiliate software tools. I went around buying up established websites like they were going out of fashion and even bought a spoof speeding fine website, and the UK's biggest forum for budgerigar owners (it was going 'cheep'!).

The only problem was, almost all of these businesses relied solely on ONE marketing pillar – one source of new customers, one place where ALL of our business came from. That pillar was SEO (Search Engine Optimisation) and had served us well for around 11 years. And then, almost overnight, Google delivered a swift, hard kick in the balls, and moved the goalposts.

 BIG IDEA...

Never rely on a SINGLE marketing pillar.

What had worked for a decade or more was suddenly ineffective. We went from being #1 for hundreds and hundreds of search terms to being relegated to page 34 of the results. From 100,000 visitors a month to fewer than 1,000. Yep, Google just "turned off" 99% of our Google when searching for our brand name!

This Google kicking was the end of the road for many of our rivals, and ness in 2011, to going back to the day job in 2013. For many, it was truly devastating, and literally the death of their business.

For me, it was the best thing that ever happened.

I'd grown complacent, totally reliant on one source of business, and assumed that things wouldn't change. I thought I knew it all, and didn't need to learn anything new. By giving me a metaphorical kick in the nuts, Google awoke me from my slumber.

Sure, I did what everyone else did in the beginning. I moaned. I whined. I complained that it was really unfair, and "how could Google do this to me?"

Waaah! Waaah! Waaah!

It was everybody's fault but mine – I mean, what had Google ever done for me, other than send me millions of highly targeted potential customers over the best part of a decade – and for FREE?

But then one day, whilst I was having a little "pity party" for myself, I asked myself what assets I had left after all the Google traffic had disappeared. And there was one business which, whilst it was still heavily reliant on the big G for new customers, had a high level of repeat custom – people bookmarked the site, and visited every day.

 BIG IDEA...

What "assets" does YOUR business own?

They typed in the web address and came back time and time again. There was a Facebook page with a few thousand "fans", and a mailing list with 14,000 people on it. So I spent some time sending emails out to that list – and that one business kept on earning a similar amount of money as it had pre-Google-kicking. And that's when it dawned on me.

They can take away my traffic, but they can't take away my mailing list.

So I put everything I had over the next six months into ONE goal – to grow that mailing list – a list that before had been an afterthought – "oh yeah, we've also got a mailing list if you want to sign up" was now the ONLY way you could gain access to the site – "You want to know what we do? Join our mailing list". And I started LEARNING again. With one swift algorithmic blow, Google made me realise that I didn't know it all. I knew very little, and it was time to go back to school.

What have you done today to get more customers?

I found myself a mentor again, I went to conferences, read books and downloaded videos. And that mailing list had doubled by the end of the year – we had survived the Google storm, but I was still juggling those 10 to 12 businesses, 8 to 10 of which had been decimated by Google.

I was only able to spend around an hour a day working on the sports betting business that, by now, was showing signs of doing better than ever before.

 BIG IDEA...

You need a MENTOR. Someone to give you clarity, advice, and a kick up the arse when you need it.

It took some frank words from my newly found mentor to make me see the bloody obvious facts that were in front of me – "What's the single biggest thing this business needs?" he said. "Oh, that's easy" I replied – "more customers!"

"OK," he said, smiling. "So... what have you done today to get more customers?"

"Well, I've been really busy today. I had a load of emails to answer for the live football business, and the accounts need doing next week, so

I've got to print off invoices, and then I'm doing the PR for the mobile phone insurance business, and speaking to the SEO guys for the travel business, and..."

"But I thought you said getting more customers for the sports betting business was THE most important thing?"

"It is, but..."

"So, what have you done TODAY to get more customers?"

"Nothing."

BIG IDEA...

You don't get a badge for being busy. You get CASH for being effective.

He smiled. I could have punched his lights out then, but instead, the lightbulb went on above my head – and in that moment I knew what needed to happen. I literally changed the structure of our businesses overnight – I sat down with Jason, my business partner, and announced: "From now on, I'm going to work full time on the sports betting business".

I think he probably thought I was just trying to shirk my responsibilities by passing the buck for all the other "stuff" that I used to do. But we totally changed things overnight. We shut down a number of the websites that were beyond saving and changed others so that they could run automatically with minimal input from us.

I would then work on the sports betting business. Jason would work on the mobile phone insurance business. And both of us had ONE job – to get and keep more customers.

That's it. As long as you've worked your profit margins out correctly, and aren't leveraging too hard using other people's money, "getting and keeping more customers" is the ONE THING that you can do – on a DAILY basis to grow your business.

To ensure that this became a daily habit, I created a "daily marketing planner" for the business – literally one side of A4 paper, which listed the things I needed to do in order to get and keep more customers:

Did one of our tips win? Craft an email to go out to the mailing list. Post a Facebook update. Send some tweets. Was it a big priced winner? If so, create a boosted post on Facebook and aim to get people onto the mailing list. Did our paid membership get good returns today? Let's put together an ad for that. Is there a big sporting event coming up in the next few weeks? If so, build a landing page and buy some traffic from Adwords.

Literally, I put together a list of things that I could do, every day with ONE purpose – to get more customers.

So, that's what I did for the next 18 months – nothing but "getting more customers". I think we quadrupled the turnover of this business in those first 18 months, and then doubled it again in the following year and a half. EIGHT times the money, from doing ONE thing in ONE business.

You are NOT Richard Branson

Before that, I was all over the place, doing 20 things in 12 businesses.

I blame Richard Branson.

Richard Branson is held up as the poster boy of entrepreneurship in the UK, so everyone thinks that if you want to be a successful entrepreneur, then you need to own a record company AND an airline. And a bank. And a radio station. And a mobile phone network. Oh, and you should also run the trains in the UK, and take on Coca-Cola in a fist-fight. All whilst bungee-jumping off buildings and sailing balloons around the world.

And I haven't even mentioned Virgin Galactic yet...

But let me make one thing very clear – you are NOT Richard Branson. Richard Branson is a freak of nature.

He's the exception, NOT the rule. Richard Branson can run 20 different business at the same time, be massively successful at them all, and look bloody cool whilst doing it.

 BIG IDEA...

You are NOT Richard Branson. Stop trying to be...

The myth of multi-tasking

For the rest of us mere mortals, however, we're much better off doing ONE THING, and doing it really, really, bloody well. For most business owners, that ONE THING should be getting and keeping customers.

I blame the myth of multi-tasking. I've lost count of the number of conversations I've had with 'Er Indoors where she's berated me for "not being able to do more than one thing at a time", and ever since I discovered the myth of multi-tasking, I've been able to reply with "Yep, you're absolutely right".

You see, there's no such thing as multi-tasking. The brain is not capable of actively focusing on anything more than one single item at a time. Sure, you can drive and listen to music. You can walk along the street and have a conversation with someone. But one of those things is always being done passively, whilst the other is active.

If you've ever been driving along listening to the radio, or a podcast (I can recommend the Big Idea Podcast!) and suddenly realised that you've driven 10 miles on autopilot, then you'll know what I mean. Or if you've had to turn the radio down so that you can concentrate on where you're going once you reach an unfamiliar part of your journey – because we all know that turning the music down allows you to see better!

Even the world's most powerful supercomputers don't multi-task.

They task-switch really effectively.

They divert their entire processing power to ONE task, complete that task in a nanosecond and then instantly move onto the next ONE task, again devoting all available resources to completing that ONE job.

See, I don't multi-task, and it turns out, neither do you. You either task-switch effectively and get shit done, or you try and get five things done at once, meaning four tasks get done passively, and you end up getting loads of things half-done, in a "f*** it, that'll do" manner, feeling completely drained and overwhelmed.

For some people though, they LOVE the badge of honour that being a "multi-tasker" gives them – they're bloody martyrs to the cause. They love nothing more than to tell you how many things they HAVE to do – TODAY – most of which could be done by someone else, but no, they love the suffering, and they love to moan about it! They'd rather do ten jobs badly than ONE job really effectively.

 BIG IDEA...

There's no such thing as EFFECTIVE multi-tasking.

These are the people who you see spending two days trying to design a flyer rather than engaging a designer for an hour or two; the people who do all the sales calls, and the customer service themselves because "no-one can do it as well as me". Then they're making the bloody product as well, updating the website, dealing with the suppliers, sending out press releases, and doing the accounts – probably all on the same day.

And then they come to us asking why they're not getting the success they want in their business.

What's your ONE THING?

One of our private clients is a perfect example of this type of manic multi-tasker – it's a husband-and-wife team, where the husband started the business a couple of decades ago, and they've now got a small team working for them. The husband is a master craftsman. He's really good at making fantastic products, but he's been allowed to drift out of that role over the years.

So he now dabbles in sales calls (which he doesn't enjoy doing, so avoids!), customer service (which he's not suited for, as he's sometimes rude to the customers!), he does the accounts (and they're a mess!), and every now and then he'll do some marketing (again reluctantly).

And the result of all this dabbling and meddling? The quality of his craftsmanship – the ONE THING that he's best at – suffers.

The first thing we did when working with them was to put a clear company structure in place, so EVERYONE in the company knew whose job it was to do sales, marketing, customer service, operations, finance, HR, quality control, etc. And the husband's role was VERY clearly defined – you make the products. It's what you're best at. It's what this company was built on.

Let the marketers talk about the care and attention to detail that you put in, let the customer service staff deal with the "pain in the arse" customers, let the financial director look after the numbers.

Meanwhile, his job is to do the ONE THING that he does best in the company. There's no multi-tasking. There's no stepping on anyone else's toes, just clearly defined roles and boundaries.

The minute he starts answering the phone and doing customer support, or sending emails out, the CEO (the wife!) can have a stern word and just say "That's not your job – you've got to do ONE THING. Make the best products you possibly can."

Whatever your role is within the company, there's likely to be ONE THING that you ultimately need to do:

- Sales – get more customers
- Marketing – get and keep more customers
- Finance – know your numbers
- HR – get and keep good staff
- Operations – make sure the systems and processes work
- Customer service – keep (or make) customers happy

- PR – get publicity
- Manual labour – make quality products/provide a good service
- Fulfilment – get the stuff there safely and on time

Sure, there'll be a multitude of tasks within that role, but just remember that you've got ONE overarching responsibility, ONE priority.

The word "priority" wasn't even pluralised until the 1940s because the very definition of the word is "the most important thing" – how on earth can multiple things ALL be THE most important? So don't ask yourself what your priorities are this week (or even what your TOP priority is) – by definition, you can only have ONE priority.

So what is it?

What's your priority?

The ONE THING that you need to do more than anything else?

Use 80/20 analysis to discover the small number of tasks that you do, that have a disproportionate effect on your sales. The things that, done correctly, by setting aside an hour or two to focus entirely on, make ALL the difference. For some that could be sending a sales email. For others, it's networking with the right people. It could be putting some effort into hiring a superstar for a particular role or creating the launch of a new product.

You're looking for the ONE THING that can act as the lead domino, knocking all those other dominoes over, creating momentum and actually getting the right stuff done in your business, or in your life.

Ask yourself this every day, and JUST do that ONE THING. Get someone else to do all the other stuff that doesn't really matter.

Every Friday, I plan out the following week on a sheet of A4 paper – there are five columns labelled Monday to Friday, and an area at the top to list the things I want to achieve that week. But at the very top, there's a bright red box, with massive capital letters that say:

"THIS WEEK'S ONE THING…"

And in that box, I write down the ONE single task that is the most important that week, something that's actually going to move my business forward, take me towards my goals, move the needle, whatever metaphor you want to use.

And I make DAMN sure that I get that ONE THING done – to the detriment of everything else. Why does it matter if I don't answer emails for a day or two if the trade-off is that I write a killer piece of sales copy that could bring in hundreds of new customers? Yes, it's easier to sort the paperwork, but I know that making 25 sales calls will bring me in the cash I need to make payroll next week.

If I ONLY achieve my ONE THING, and nothing else – I've beaten the week.

And believe me, there are weeks where that is literally all I do – during school holidays etc., I enter family mode, and maybe only grab a half day in the office. So I've got to make that time count by doing something important. "Inbox zero" ain't important (Your inbox is just everyone else's to-do list). Maintaining progress towards your goals is.

As well as the weekly ONE THING, I'll then have a daily ONE THING, which I'll write on my planner at the top of that day, and then draw a line under, before listing the rest of the "stuff" that I want to do that day. That line acts as a mental barrier, telling me "until you've done your ONE THING, do not pass Go, do not collect £200". Once I've done my ONE THING, I've beaten the day, and can move on to the "other stuff" – even if I waste the rest of the day checking emails and dicking around on Facebook, I've still beaten the day, I've still made progress towards my goals, I've still got the important stuff done.

How can you make the boat go faster?

Make doing the ONE THING a habit every day, and over the long-term, you'll find that you can achieve things that you never thought possible. Take the example of the Team GB men's Eights rowing team from the late '90s and early 2000s.

They were pretty consistent – they finished seventh in just about every championships – Commonwealth Games, Olympics, you name it. And in 1998, they once again finished seventh in the Commonwealth Games, meaning that yet again, they missed out on the final (the top six would go on to compete for the medals), and as part of the debrief they pondered what it would take for them to break into the top six.

From seventh to sixth is a MUCH bigger jump than you might think (hence they hadn't been able to break that glass ceiling despite training hard, working hard, eating right, and giving their all during the race), so one of the team members said "hell, if we're talking about making crazy goals that are completely unachievable, how about we go for the gold medal?"

Once they'd finished falling about laughing, they then gave it some serious thought. To go from a consistent seventh-best to the best in the world would not take a small improvement. 10% extra wouldn't cut it. They couldn't just copy what the top six did, as they needed to be BETTER, not the same. That's when they decided that they needed to extend the "competition mode" – that time when they were in the zone, 100% focused on the competition ahead of them, to the detriment of everything else.

Usually, their training built up, and built up, until with about three months to go before the event, they'd enter "competition mode", where winning that race was the ONE THING that they thought about, the thing that affected every decision they made.

"If we're going to stand a chance of winning a medal, we need to start competition mode NOW."

Silence.

The team members worked this through. Why not? It would mean two years of intense focus on ONE THING, but many of them were heading towards the end of their careers, and Sydney 2000 was likely to be their last chance to win an Olympic medal. Two years of competition mode though?

One by one, the team raised their hands – "I'm in. Let's win ourselves a medal."

They briefed their coach, who got on board almost immediately, and told them that for the next two years, they only had to worry about ONE THING...

Making the boat go faster.

Every single decision that every team member made for the next two years had to be filtered through that same question.

Shall I go out for a curry and pint next Friday? Will it make the boat go faster? No. Bugger.

It's 5am on a freezing Sunday in February. Should I give training a miss today? Will it make the boat go faster? No.

Should I have that difficult conversation with a team member who isn't pulling his weight? Will it make the boat go faster? Right, I'm on it.

They literally lived their lives by this ONE THING for the best part of two years, even missing the opening ceremony of the games, watching it on the TV in their room because attending would have meant 90 minutes on a coach, another 90 minutes on their feet, when they couldn't control their nutrition, and they'd get at least an hour's less sleep – that wasn't going to make their boat go faster, was it!

Every single person on that team knew what their ONE THING was – it was to make their boat go faster – just like the cleaner, sweeping the corridors at NASA in the 1960s who was interviewed by President Nixon on a tour, and asked: "What do you do around here?"

His answer?

"I'm helping to put a man on the moon, Mr President."

He knew his ONE THING.

In the same way, the GOLD MEDAL WINNING Team GB men's Eights rowers knew their ONE THING.

Do YOU?

Be like a postage stamp. Stick to ONE THING until you get there.

 BIG IDEA...

"Will it make the boat go faster?"

MAGIC INGREDIENT #2 – DESIRE
(A.K.A. DESIRE GETS SHIT DONE...)

"I'll tell you what I want, what I really, really want
So tell me what you want, what you really, really want
I'll tell you what I want, what I really, really want
So tell me what you want, what you really, really want
I wanna, I wanna, I wanna, I wanna
I wanna really, really, really wanna zigazig ah"

The Spice Girls
Wannabe

We can all create amazing-sounding GOALS that will really stretch and move our businesses forward, but how do you improve your chances of ACHIEVING them? You have to link the GOALS to your DESIRE.

Want to lose two stone in three months? That's an admirable target. But ultimately, your DESIRE to hit that goal will determine whether you're willing to put the work in, week-in, week-out, day-after-day, to actually achieve it.

Which do you DESIRE more – a six-pack or a cupcake? If the answer is truthfully a six-pack, then you need to understand that cupcakes are treasonous to your GOALS –not just a bad idea, they're bloody treasonous. And if you don't feel that strongly about it, then your DESIRE for the GOAL isn't high enough. You don't have a GOAL. You have a dream. And you won't achieve anything by dreaming.

Desire for change can lead to a big idea.

Jump in the DeLorean with me again, and let's take a trip in time, back to the beginning of 2000. I was five years into my "career" as a civil servant, and had just been subjected to an enforced change of department – the job I enjoyed was whipped out from beneath me, and replaced with one where I was cold-calling "absent parents" for the CSA chasing them for money.

I was no longer working with the team I'd spent the last three years with – I wasn't even in the same building. I knew next to nobody in this new building and I'm now a poorly-paid debt collector for the government. The average "life expectancy" for someone to stay in the CSA at the time was two years – in my previous role, it was 20! I think it took me less than a fortnight to realise that I needed to find a way out ASAP.

I would go into work and I would enjoy the commute more than I would enjoy actually sitting at my desk. I would just sit there and I would wish the time away. I'd look at the clock and work out how many minutes it was before I could actually leave, how many seconds it was before I could clock off. I'd get my calculator out and work out, "How much am I being paid to be here? How much am I wasting per hour here?"

It even got to the point where I took up smoking again – I'd quit about nine months before, and I started back on the cancer sticks again within a month of starting the new job, just so I could get five minutes away from my desk in the morning for a cigarette break, and another five minutes off in the afternoon. It would end up being another six years before I quit for good, so this isn't something I'd recommend for any clock-watchers out there!

Something had to give – we'd recently bought our first house, and were planning to get married the following year. 'Er Indoors was at uni, so she only had a part-time wage – money was tight. I applied for several other jobs, without success – no-one looked favourably on a 22-year old who wanted to quit a role he'd only been in for a matter of months.

This was the height of the dotcom boom though, and people like Sean Parker, Ernst Malmsten, Brent Hoberman and Martha Lane Fox were being held up as heroes for launching websites like Napster, boo.com and lastminute.com. Every day would see a new dotcom millionaire splashed over the pages of the newspapers and magazines – many of these guys were a similar age to me, and some of them just had an idea – not even a fully functional website, just an idea! So naturally, I thought "Maybe I could do that."

There was only one slight problem with that. I didn't have access to the internet, or a computer, or an idea.

But what I did have was...

DESIRE.

How desire helped me quit my job

I had an absolute burning passion to quit the civil service, that was getting stronger and stronger every week I endured there. So I spent a lot of time at Sarah's parents' house, as they had both a computer and the internet (Freeserve pay-as-you-go dial-up if my memory serves me right!), so all I needed then was the idea.

I'd waste my days clock watching, day-dreaming of ideas that I could do – most of them were awful – either just rip-offs of what other people were already doing or just stuff that nobody would ever use in a million years. I registered about four or five domain names, which these days doesn't seem much as they only cost around £5, but back in 2000, I think I was paying something like £60 for each one.

 BIG IDEA

How badly do you want it?

I had Crapster.co.uk (a rip-off of Napster, which was HUGE at the time), KingJohn.co.uk (which was my online pseudonym for a good couple of years!), and a couple of others that I can't remember.

I recall one day having "a brilliant name" for an online auction site like eBay – I would call it GoingGoing.com. I rushed home that evening to register it, only to find that it had been snapped up the day before – by Brent Hoberman no less. I took this as a sign that I was on the right path, and coupled with my DESIRE to be free from the day job, I borrowed some money to buy my first computer and set up internet access at home.

Eventually, it dawned on me that simply "having ideas" and registering domain names wasn't leading to Silicon Valley VC funds hammering on my door waving massive cheques at me, and I needed to actually get a website up. Only one problem with that.

I didn't have the first clue how to build a website.

So I taught myself. I went out and bought "Building Websites for Dummies", and read it in my lunch hours. I would come home from working eight hours for the CSA and put in another four or five-hour shift on "my" business. I'd literally get out of bed in the morning, work for a few hours on the website, do a 1pm to 9pm shift in the CSA, and then come home, have some food and go to work on my website from 10pm until 1 or 2am in the morning.

Without that really strong DESIRE, there's no way I'd have jumped over the hurdles that were in my way, hurdles that were stopping me from launching the business. I'd have given up, thinking it was too tough, and that it just wasn't meant to be.

Instead, I carried on working four or five hours a day on top of the day job for 18 months without earning a single penny. I had to teach myself how to code, how to get traffic to the site, how to set up email, how to monetise the traffic, how to get the traffic coming back – all for free, and on top of my normal job.

Fast forward to April 2001, and I received my very first cheque – for £13.51. I didn't know whether to cash it or frame it – in hindsight, I wish I'd chosen the latter, but I needed the money at the time! That just stoked the DESIRE further, as I knew that making money from this WAS possible – I just needed to scale it up.

So I started putting in seven or eight hours a day on top of the day job, working through the weekends, and even taking annual leave so I could work full time on the website for a week. I may even have taken the odd "sick" day when I couldn't face going into the CSA, and I had the much more appealing option of working towards MY goals.

And then it happened. I got another cheque. And another. And another. By the summer of 2001, I was earning as much from the website as I was from the day job. But it still wasn't the "safe secure job" that the Civil Service offered, so I wasn't able to quit immediately.

I was able to go part time though – I now only worked three days a week for the CSA, leaving me free to focus 100% on my business on Mondays and Thursdays (oh and Saturdays and Sundays, and for six or seven hours on a Tuesday, Wednesday and Friday). I noticed the difference almost immediately – that extra time spent working on MY business rather than pushing papers around for the government had a huge impact, and by the end of my first month as a part-timer, I was earning twice as much from my business as I was from my salary.

That made my DESIRE to leave even stronger, as now I was not only doing a job I hated, but it was actually COSTING me money to go there. I'd sit there watching the seconds tick by on the clock, get my government-issued calculator out, and work out how much more I would have been earning if I was sat at home growing my business.

I lasted just three months as a part-timer before quitting altogether. I would have left after two, but the bastards made me work my month's notice – jobsworths! I've got this cute little calendar sat on my desk, which is set to Monday 31st December 2001.

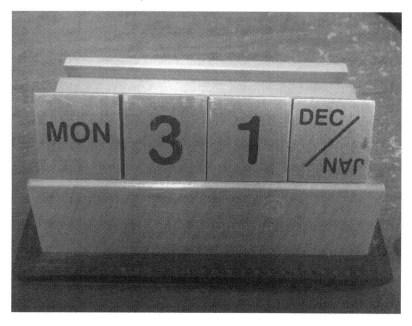

That was the last day that I had a REAL job. The last day I was answerable to someone else.

The last day I was paid "by the hour" rather than by the value I give. I keep it on my desk to remind me that being my own boss – doing what I want, when I want, where I want, how I want, is what's REALLY important to me (above the cars, houses and holidays on the DESIRE scale), and it's a reminder not to do anything that could land me back in the land of the employed (though I'm probably pretty much unemployable now I would say!).

Why do I need reminding of this? Doc's waiting for us in the DeLorean again; this time we're just going to jump forward a few years to 2004, and find out what happens when you run your business following someone else's DESIRE, not your own...

Living the dream A.K.A: my personal nightmare

So, it's 2004 now – I've been running my first business (a website listing places to find freebies and competitions on the internet) full time for the last two years. We've grown quite nicely, and I now employ two people, and recently launched a second business (doing Google Adwords for clients – we literally started using Adwords the day it launched in the UK!). Life was good.

But then we started listening to the wrong people. We started hanging around with other internet marketing folks, most of whom were really nice, genuine, down to earth people. But one or two were INCREDIBLY money-driven. If you weren't earning £100k a month back then, you weren't trying hard enough was their attitude.

They wanted a £100m business, skyscrapers, fast cars, country estates, yachts, you name it. That was their DESIRE. And I thought it was mine too. So I started going off chasing the big money, by massively scaling up our nice little setup.

Over the course of around three months, we went from having two businesses, run by three members of staff (all working from home), to having at least twenty different businesses, run by fifteen members of staff, over two offices.

And I HATED it.

I didn't want to manage a large team. I felt that, almost overnight, I'd gone from being an entrepreneur to being an HR manager. I no longer had the time to devote to the stuff that I loved doing (and that I knew worked!) because I was so busy sorting out staff issues, like replacing the fridge, unblocking the staff toilet, dealing with lazy, unmotivated employees, sorting out who had said what to whom, and who was sleeping with whom.

That led to, a real lack of DESIRE.

I'd gone from, "I really, really want / need to be running my own business" to "I THINK I want to have a 100 million pound a year business, I want 100 members of staff. I want the skyscraper. I want the fast cars. I want the yacht and the private jet."

Actually, no. I didn't want that. But I was hanging around with people who did. Who you hang around with makes a huge difference to your values and beliefs. In 2002 and 2003 I was living the dream. In 2004 and 2005, I was living SOMEONE ELSE'S dream. Well, that was my nightmare.

My lack of DESIRE got so bad, that I actually walked away from it all in the summer of 2005.

The business that I'd launched five years earlier was now unrecognisable to me, and certainly wasn't the sort of business that I wanted to run. I simply couldn't stand to work there any more than I could have gone back to working at the CSA.

In hindsight, I should have been confident enough to recognise this, and do whatever was necessary – it was my business after all. But I didn't want to sack a load of people and shut down loads of businesses. I felt that it probably would work out, but just not with me. I developed ostrich syndrome and just buried my head in the sand, hoping it would all be ok.

It wasn't.

We ran out of money about 12 months later, and I was forced to return to the business. I literally HAD to. I would have lost both the business and my house if I hadn't.

 BIG IDEA...

Don't HOPE that things will get better, CHANGE THINGS so that they do.

Most of the staff had left "organically" shall we say, as it was such a horrible, toxic place to work at the time. My first act upon returning was to sack half the remaining staff and shut down both of the offices.

This was truly horrible to have to do, and a big reason why I never want to let myself get into that position again.

We entered survival mode. We had very little money coming in, zero cash to pay the bills with, and a choice every single month of "do we pay the VAT bill, or the payroll this month?" (and many months there wasn't enough cash to pay EITHER of them!).

What kept me going?

DESIRE.

All of a sudden now, the DESIRE was, "I'm not going to lose my house. I'm not going to go bankrupt here. I'm not going to lose everything. Let's max out the credit cards. Let's go without pay for six months. Let's work 100-hour weeks. Let's do whatever is necessary to survive."

 BIG IDEA...

Are you willing to do WHATEVER'S NECESSARY to succeed?

If the DESIRE to survive wasn't there, if I actually didn't care, if it didn't really matter to me if the business went under, if I didn't care that people I'd worked closely with, and become friends with would lose their jobs, then I wouldn't have been motivated to do half of that stuff, but because the DESIRE to survive was so strong, I was willing to do whatever was necessary.

What Lord Sugar taught me about raising children

My DESIRE changed once again when I had kids. I remember sitting in an MOT garage about four months after Jack, my eldest, was born in 2009. I had an hour to kill whilst I waited for my car and was reading Alan Sugar's biography. Despite everything that had happened just a few years earlier, I was still hero-worshipping guys like Lord Sugar and Richard Branson – people who had built HUGE corporations, with hundreds of staff.

Even then, I still thought that what I really wanted was a big business, until I read one line in Lord Sugar's book...

"I never really saw my kids much when they were growing up."

That hit me like a bloody sledgehammer. There I was, a new dad, hero-worshipping a guy who didn't spend any time with his kids. And then I recalled reading something similar in Richard Branson's autobiography 'Losing My Virginity' – "I wasn't really around much for Holly and Sam when they were little."

In that moment, I knew I'd started living someone else's dream again. What I REALLY wanted was to be there for my kids throughout their lives. I want to be the dad who's there at every sports day, every assembly, doing the school run, and just playing with them and spending time with them – THAT'S what was important to me.

I didn't want them saying "my dad's really successful. I read so on his LinkedIn profile" when they're older. I had an argument with a fellow entrepreneur once, who asked me for advice on how to fill the "wasted time" doing the school runs. I replied that spending time with your children is NEVER wasted time. He just didn't get it though, probably because he has different beliefs and DESIRES to me – my DESIRE to build my businesses around my family is so strong, it's ingrained in everything I do, and every decision I make, especially where my children are concerned.

Can't is a four letter word

My kids will tell you that I've banned the word "can't" from our household. As far as I'm concerned, "can't" is a four-letter word. Don't tell me you "can't" do your homework. Be honest with me (and yourself), and tell me "it's hard, and I don't want to do it" – because you CAN do it. You ARE capable. But you offer up "I can't do it" as an automatic response to things that are hard.

The only time I'll allow my kids to use "can't" is when they literally are unable to do something. And even then, I make them add a word to the statement – "yet".

So, "I can't ride a bike" becomes "I can't ride a bike yet".

"I can't read" becomes "I can't read yet".

"I can't speak Spanish" becomes "I can't speak Spanish yet."

 **BIG IDEA...**

Don't be a can't.

So if you're telling yourself that you "can't do public speaking", ask yourself whether you should actually be saying "I can't do public speaking yet" or "I don't want to do public speaking".

DESIRE is what keeps you going when your willpower runs out. Remember, willpower is a finite resource and it doesn't last long. Anyone who's stepped foot in a gym in January will know that it's full of people amped up on willpower – "New Year, New Me!" and all that bollocks. But by mid-February, they're all gone, willpower depleted. They're back on the sofa watching TV and eating pizza.

Unless, of course, their DESIRE to change is high enough to combat the willpower metre running low when it's dark and cold outside, they feel like crap, and are still aching from the last workout – those moments when going to the gym, or eating healthily is the last thing you want to do – only a really strong DESIRE will keep you on track.

Everything has a price.

Desire is how much you're willing to pay.

LIFE'S TOO SHORT...

"You'll live to dance another day
it's just now you'll have to dance, for the two of us,
so stop looking so damn depressed and sing with all
your heart that the Queen is dead"

Frank Turner, "Long Live the Queen"

It's my sister's 51st birthday tomorrow. Well, technically it's not, as she died many years ago, so she'll always be 35 years old. I was her baby brother – eleven years, six months and one day younger than her, yet as I sit here writing this now, I'm four years older than she will ever be.

Any plans that Linda made for old age, for retirement, for travel, for all the things she was going to do with the kids when they grew up – they all went out the window one night in 2001 when she died suddenly in her sleep, leaving behind two devastated young children and changing the lives of all those who were close to her.

Her death affected all of us greatly and continues to influence me now, even a decade and a half later. It is the reason that I now live very much in the present. I'm very conscious, because of what happened to Linda, that you can make all these plans for the future, but if you keep putting stuff off until "one day", there is a possibility that day may never come.

How many days do you have left – and what are you going to do with them?

The average life expectancy for a male in the UK is currently 81 years. That means that I'm going to experience something like 29,500 days in my lifetime – and I've already seen 14,500 of them – so that means I've got less than 15,000 days left to do EVERYTHING that I want to do.

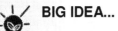
The sun will rise and fall 15,000 more times before I take my last breath (if I live to be average – and I don't plan on being average...

I want to live till I'm 120, and experience space travel in my lifetime, so there'll be no sitting in the rocking chair for 20 years then shuffling off for me if I have my way), and once I'm gone, the sun will continue to rise and fall for everyone else – but my turn will be over.

I plan on having some FUN whilst it's still my turn!

Nobody knows exactly how many days they've got left on the planet, and whilst I'm always making plans for the future (I've already mentioned my 20-year business plans) – if you look at my vision board for this year, you will see that there are lots of business and investment goals that I want to achieve – you'll also see a hell of a lot of fun that I want to have – right now.

Not "one day", not "in a few years", but now. This year. In a couple of months. Next week. Right NOW. Let's not wait. Let's take the kids to Walt Disney World this year. Let's buy a car that's bloody good fun to drive, and then book in some track days with it. Let's travel the world, and see the best bands in the world playing live.

Life's a journey, not a destination, as the old saying goes – and that journey started decades ago, so why are you STILL putting stuff off? Why not design your business around the lifestyle you want RIGHT NOW?

The kids are just about old enough to enjoy Disney (and put up with the Florida heat), so we're taking them – first opportunity. They're also just about old enough to learn to ski, so we've booked in skiing lessons for this year, with a view to taking them out on the slopes next year.

We're putting nothing off until "one day" because I know that Linda's "one day" never came.

Lots of people's "one days" never come.

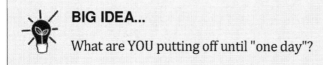
"I'm sorry, you've only got six months..."

Ricardo Semler is someone whose "one day" very nearly didn't come. He's a Brazilian entrepreneur who took his family company, Semco from revenues of $4m to $232m in a couple of years. He was diagnosed with cancer and was told there was a 50% chance that it would be terminal.

He had this awful limbo period of a couple of days whilst he waited for the outcome of the biopsy, basically waiting to hear whether he would live or die. Eventually, he was called into the doctor's office, where he was told "Good news. You're in remission. You've got the all-clear."

Ricardo knew in an instant that he had dodged a bullet, and from that moment on, it changed the way he lived his life. He now spends two days per week enjoying what he calls "Terminal Days" – for those two days every week, he lives those days as though he HAD received that terminal diagnosis he dreaded when he went into the doctor's office.

It sounds morbid, but it serves as a reminder of just how close he came to actually dying. We've all heard the cliché about "living each day as if it's your last" but that's not something people can actually do realistically, as, if it really WAS your last day on earth. You could give away all your money, tell everyone on the planet exactly what you think of them, and act completely without regard for consequences or the law. But you certainly wouldn't want to spend the day working your arse off, accumulating all sorts of possessions that you're never going to use, or focusing on getting richer and richer – as Warren Buffett's good friend and mentor famously said:

"Who wants to be the richest man in the graveyard?"

Benjamin Graham

Regrets – I've had a few...

What Ricardo's "Terminal Days" allow him to do are to do the sort of things that one might do if given only a few months to live – enjoying sunsets, dancing in the rain, writing that book, making sure your kids know you love them, doing the little things that, if you were sat in that doctor's office and you were told "I'm sorry, but you've only got three months left", what the hell would you do (apart from blow all your money on cocaine and hookers – doing that two days a week won't end well!)

The top five greatest regrets of the dying are:

1. "I wish I'd lived a life true to myself, not to what others expected of me"

2. "I wish I hadn't worked so hard"

3. "I wish I'd had the courage to express my feelings"

4. "I wish I'd stayed in touch with my friends"

5. "I wish I'd let myself be happier"

Does any of this hit home with you?

Are you living an awesome life on Facebook, but not so much in real life? Are you still hitting the "hustle", pulling all-nighters and working yourself into the ground? (even after reading chapter one of this book, which told you NOT to?).

Do you bottle up your feelings to protect other people from getting hurt, or feeling upset, even to the point where it makes you feel strong resentment towards them?

Have you lost contact with your friends, or do you find you have hundreds of "virtual" friends on social media, but that you're actually less "social" than you were pre-Facebook, and have very few REAL friends who you can phone up and yap to for an hour or two?

And the last one – "letting yourself be happy" – sounds really obvious doesn't it? I certainly found it surprising that it was in the top five, but there are indeed hundreds of thousands of people who don't realise until it's too late that happiness is a choice you can make. Fear of change, and of what other people will think (see regret #1) is the main reason that people don't choose to be happy.

On the surface, many of those people ought to have been happy – they had all the material possessions they could wish for, they'd achieved everything they set out to in life, and in many cases were heralded as a shining example of personal success, but they died feeling unfulfilled, and unhappy.

Achievement versus fulfilment

So many people chase these huge goals and then die unhappy because they haven't lived a life of fulfilment. There was a brilliant interview I heard with Tony Robbins recently, in which he talked about the death of the amazing comedian and actor Robin Williams. You can see a snippet of it at:

https://www.youtube.com/watch?v=euW991ev2y0

Robbins says that Robin Williams was a perfect example of someone who was chasing (and achieving) these really ambitious goals, chasing achievement after achievement, thinking it would make him happy, but ultimately leaving him unfulfilled.

He said he wanted his own TV show. He achieved it.

He wanted the number one TV show. He did it.

He wanted a beautiful family. He got it.

He wanted more money that he knew how to spend. He got it.

He wanted to go to Hollywood and make movies. He did that.

He wanted to win an Oscar. He did it.

He wanted to win another Oscar, for NOT being funny (the main thing he was known for). He did that.

He wanted the whole world to love him. He did it.

And he hanged himself.

Was Robin Williams successful? That depends on your definition of the word "successful" doesn't it? Because if you look at material things, the possessions he gained, the money he earned, the awards he won, the adulation that he attracted, the achievements that he made, in every sense of the word – yes, he was successful.

But was he happy?

Was he fulfilled?

Maybe not.

And if you're not happy, and you're not fulfilled, can you truly call yourself successful?

 BIG IDEA...

Are you chasing achievements rather than FULFILMENT?

I implore you – live a life without regrets. My sister won't get a tomorrow. Robin Williams won't get a tomorrow. You or I may not get a tomorrow. No-one knows when our time has come, so please don't keep putting stuff off until "one day". There are still several things on my "bucket list" that I would like to do that I haven't got around to yet. There are places in the world that I still want to see. I want to go to Australia, I want to see Canada, and Alaska, and Greece, and Italy, and California, and... and...

I can't squeeze them all in right now, but rest assured that I'm ticking them off one-by-one over the next few years as soon as I'm physically able to – I'm not putting anything off for a minute longer than I have to – nothing's waiting until retirement. So many of our clients say "oh, that's fine – I'll travel in 20 years when I retire" – well, what happens if you die in 15 years, having never done it?

Why spend 40 years (or more like 50 years now!) working your arse off, just to delay all the fun stuff to the end of your life, when your energy reserves are low, your joints creak every time you get out of a chair, and the highlight of your day is watching Countdown every afternoon?

You've only got one life, so live it without regrets.

MAGIC INGREDIENT #3 – KNOWLEDGE
(A.K.A. WHAT YOU LEARN AFTER YOU KNOW IT ALL...)

"We are all born ignorant, but one must work hard to remain stupid."

Benjamin Franklin

Have you ever been to a REALLY big library? Somewhere like the British Library in London, which is the second biggest library in the world, containing something like 14 million books.

I love libraries, as I see every single book as documenting somebody's life – a person who achieved something, who actually did something of note, something suitably astounding that they were compelled to write a book about it, so that future generations could read exactly how and why they did it.

It's one of the reasons I decided to write this book – not because I've achieved anything so earth-shatteringly stunning that I need to pass it on to future generations but because I've managed to achieve SOME success, which many would define as being a decent level, without really working that hard, being that intelligent, and definitely without being born with a silver spoon in my mouth – and whilst I see many other people working harder and harder, yet getting nowhere, still on their hamster wheels, I wondered what the difference between us was.

The difference is KNOWLEDGE.

"John must try harder"

I can't remember exactly when I fell out of love with learning, but it was at some point during secondary school. I still have fond memories of junior school, when I would soak up information like a sponge – I loved school, and it showed in my grades.

Life in secondary school started along these same lines, but at some point, the teachers who had ignited this passion for learning, who had inspired and encouraged me, were replaced with others who were more concerned with their own targets, based their teaching style on the drill sergeant from Full Metal Jacket, didn't really enjoy teaching, and in some cases just didn't like me.

I still achieved fairly decent grades at GCSE (including an 'A' in Business Studies, where my end of year report for 1993 reported that I "showed a real aptitude for the subject" – go me!), but there was a common theme in many of my reports from other subjects by then:

> "The exam result whilst satisfactory for most is, in fact, disappointing for John and I expect higher grades to be achieved next year."

> "Work handed in is below what he is capable of achieving."

> "It's a shame John doesn't always maintain this level of performance."

> "John is not without ability, but he has a laid-back attitude to his work."

> "Much potential is evident – how far he goes is up to John himself. I hope he has the drive."

I'd entered the secondary school system as a bright-eyed, bushy-tailed newbie, eager to learn, and eager to please. And within a few years I was still technically capable of producing work of a high standard, but that school had completely killed my love of learning – to the point that I took my two 'A's and nine 'B's at GCSE, and went out into the real world, a move that I'm sure must have disappointed my parents.

They had moved house so that we'd be in the catchment area for that school. They'd recognised early on that I had a very high interest in learning and seemed to do well when pushed and motivated at school.

They were already planning my graduation ceremony in their heads I'm sure, as I was destined to be the very first Lamerton in our family to attend university. (That honour went to my niece Eloise instead, who studied Forensic Science at Bristol's University of West England.)

Want a job in the civil service? Download the blueprints.

Instead, I took a summer job at the local job centre, and given a taste of the real world, decided that I simply couldn't face another two years of "learning" at that school. I took a YTS (youth training scheme) apprenticeship within the job centre, which paid me the grand sum of £29.50 per week. But for me, it wasn't about the money – it was about what I could learn from the job centre. Who knows what employers are looking for better than anyone? The people writing the job ads for them of course!

I spent hours every day speaking to business owners and employers, finding out exactly what they wanted from their prospective employees – and they told me time and again that they wanted to experience, and really good attitudes.

"What about an A-level in Business Studies?" I'd ask.

"What about it?" would be the answer I'd get.

Turns out that apprenticeship was worth its weight in gold – I was able to use everything I'd learnt (and the contacts I'd built up) there, to spend three months working in Portugal as a translator before returning to the UK and getting the heads-up that the local Benefits Agency would be hiring admin officers shortly, and that I should be sure to apply.

Several of my colleagues vetted my application form for me, ensured my CV was polished and prepped me on what the interview panel was likely to be looking for.

I was warned not to get my hopes up:

1. I was only 17.

2. The highlights of my CV thus far were six months working as an apprentice and three months in Portugal.

3. I was applying for a government post that was a "level 2" job. Normally, I'd be expected to apply for a role as an admin assistant first, and then work my way up to a promotion to admin officer after a few years.

4. More than 2,000 people were expected to apply, and there were only 14 roles.

Bollocks to that – I got the job!

Looking back now, I can see that the reason I got the job (when common sense would dictate that the odds were very much against me) was because I'd stumbled across the blueprint – I'd infiltrated the Civil Service via the YTS scheme, and used it to work out exactly how someone like me, who was completely unqualified for the job, could land it anyway.

 BIG IDEA...

Knowledge allows you to "reverse engineer" someone else's success to plan your own.

The knowledge of what to say, how to interview, what the interviewers would be looking for, what to put on my CV, how to appear "older than my years", how to compensate for the lack of action on my CV, this was all knowledge that I used to my advantage – I literally downloaded the "how to get a job in the Civil Service" blueprint, by speaking to 10 or 15 people who had done exactly that.

Not that I put it down to that at the time though – oh no! What had happened was clearly the recruitment panel for the Benefits Agency had recognised the raw talent in me, and had decided to fast-track this superstar, who would spend a year or two as an admin officer before the first in a succession of promotions that would ultimately see me running the entire department by the time I was 30.

Didn't QUITE work out that way, did it...

If you're looking to become a doctor, or an architect, or a lawyer, you need to get a formal education. For a lot of people though, they'd be far better off designing their own curriculum, learning the skills that they need, to perform at the highest level in their chosen field. I've seen so many people do a couple of years of A-levels, followed by a university degree, only to end up flipping burgers because they didn't know what they wanted to do with their lives, and so ended up wasting those years taking irrelevant higher education courses.

These kids are then saddled with huge student debts for their worthless degrees, often in subjects that are no longer relevant for the world we now live in (never mind the world we will live in in 10 years' time, once millions of human jobs are lost forever to automation).

As TV producer Mike Rowe said in a recent interview:

> *"We're giving unlimited piles of money we don't have, to people who will never be able to pay it back, training them for jobs that no longer exist."*

What will you learn AFTER you know it all?

John Wooden was a legendary UCLA basketball coach back in the 1960s – his teams won 10 NCAA Championships (including SEVEN in a row), so he knows a thing or two about not only achieving success but staying at the top of your game. As he told all of his students:

> *"It's what you learn AFTER you know it all that counts the most."*

Getting to the top is tough, but not impossible. Staying at the top is REALLY hard. Whilst success is addictive, and you can find yourself always chasing more (like Robin Williams did as mentioned in the last chapter), success also comes with its own built-in trap, ready to swallow up those who fall for it.

"It is very easy... to believe you have all of the answers, especially when you begin to enjoy some success."

What Coach Wooden was striving for, what the best teams and the best businesses are striving for, what I'm striving for, and what you should be striving for – is constant, never-ending improvement.

To always be learning. Every day's a school day. Becoming the best you can be is a journey, not a destination.

I fell into this exact trap myself – when I first started the business. I knew that I knew nothing, and so I spent a lot of time learning. (It's kind of hard to run an internet marketing business otherwise when you know NOTHING about either the internet or marketing...) But after a few years, I started having some success, and naively thought I'd "made it" – I not only stopped reading, stopped learning, but even used to mock those who did read personal development books.

As far as I was concerned, I knew it all. There was precisely nothing that any of these authors, coaches or mentors could teach me – they were all just out to fleece me of my money, to line their own pockets at my expense. I must have gone six or seven years without reading a single nonfiction book. Then Google gave me a kick up the arse.

I didn't need to know anything else, because I knew how to get my website ranked #1 on Google, for some pretty tasty terms. Until April 2012, when Google moved the goalposts – massively – so much so they were not even in the same city, let alone the same stadium. I suddenly went from being #1 on Google to being on page 586. From having 10,000 free, highly targeted visitors to my website per month to... erm... none.

Overnight.

That was the moment I realised I DIDN'T know everything after all – and it was the moment I sought out a mentor. Even then, I didn't think they could help me that much. I recall sitting down with them and pretty much telling them that I knew ALMOST everything I needed to, but maybe they could help me squeeze an extra 20% out of my business.

 BIG IDEA...

You DON'T know it all. Don't think for a moment that you do.

What they did was light a fire underneath me – I realised VERY quickly that not only did I not know EVERYTHING, but that I actually barely knew ANYTHING. In that moment, I was transported back to the very start of my business career, when I knew that I knew nothing, and I started learning ferociously again – consuming book after book after book, taking training courses, and listening to podcasts and audiobooks. I'd book one-to-one training with experts, took on a personal mentor, and crucially, implemented all that I'd learnt.

And instead of squeezing an extra 20% out of my business, I grew it by 400% over the next 18 months, taking it to a level that I never ever dreamed of – doing things that I never even knew existed.

You don't know what you don't know.

That was the key difference between my first bout of learning and my second – the first time I had a final destination in mind, so I learnt ONLY what I needed to in order to get there. And when I got there, I stopped.

When I started learning again, I also learnt the importance of CONTINUING to learn, as a life skill. The most successful people in virtually any field you care to mention aren't simply sat at the top writing books and selling courses – they're still reading books and taking courses. They're still learning.

They have that thirst for knowledge, that desire to always be learning, to always be a better version of yourself today than you were yesterday. And that's what I've carried on now. Not a day goes by that I don't learn something – I've always got a podcast in my ear, a Kindle in my hand, and a training course in the diary.

Every day's a school day. You can choose to bunk off if you like – there'll be no truant officer coming to speak to your parents or drag you back to the classroom. But to paraphrase that old teacher classic – "It's your own life you're wasting..."

DO YOU KNOW YOUR ASSET FROM YOUR ELBOW?

"The number one problem in today's generation, and economy is the lack of financial literacy."

Alan Greenspan
Chairman of the Federal Reserve of the
United States from 1987 to 2006

One of the very first personal development books I read when I first started my business back in 2000, was "Rich Dad, Poor Dad" by Robert T. Kiyosaki. The lessons learnt in that book stayed with me for many years, and I've probably re-read it seven or eight times over the last seventeen years.

In it, Kiyosaki tells the story of his two "dads" growing up in Hawaii – one, his actual father, was a highly educated government worker, who was telling the young Kiyosaki to work hard at school, get good grades, and then get a nice safe, secure job with a good pension. This was the path that he himself had taken, and Kiyosaki could see that it hadn't worked out particularly well for his old man – Kiyosaki Senior had worked hard for over 40 years, and had very little to show for it. This was his poor dad.

The importance of financial literacy

His "rich" dad was actually his best friend Mike's father. In contrast to his own father, Mike's dad didn't seem to work particularly hard, left school with no qualifications, and yet he was one of the richest men in Hawaii – because instead of "getting a good job", Mike's dad had focused on becoming a really good businessman and investor – and he was passing that knowledge onto Mike.

He also agreed to take Robert under his wing, and soon, Kiyosaki found that his "rich" dad's thinking was the complete polar opposite of his own father's. Mike's dad taught Robert and Mike to become financially literate, to know what numbers were important, to be able to read a balance sheet (both for their personal finances as well as for companies), to know the difference between an asset and a liability, and to be confident in understanding and talking about money, and numbers in general.

Most business owners I meet these days aren't financially literate and have no interest in becoming so. You don't need to be Carol Vorderman, poring over the company accounts on a daily basis, but you should have a handle on the key numbers that tell you if your business, investments, or household is making, or losing money – and if so, what to do about it. Too many small business owners want to leave all the numbers to the accountant – and that may actually make sense if you've got an in-house financial director (FD) to delegate to, but even then, you should be financially literate enough that you can have a conversation with them regularly, and actually understand what they're telling you.

If you don't have your own FD, delegation by abstinence, by way of leaving everything financial to an accountant who you maybe see once or twice a year, and when you DO see them, you don't understand a word of what they say– that's a recipe for disaster. At the very least, I believe you should be able to have a conversation with your accountant on a monthly basis about the key numbers within the business – don't wait until they've done your year-end accounts. What use is it them telling you what happened in the business a year ago? What can you possibly do with that information? You want to know what's happening right now – which products provide you with the best margins? Which marketing channels are delivering amazing ROIs? Do you need to invest in more robust systems, take on additional staff, or reduce your overheads?

Yet going back a few years, this is exactly how we used to work! If Jason (my business partner) called me up and asked how the numbers were looking, my answer would be something like "I don't know. The accountant hasn't delivered the management accounts yet. I'll let you know in three months' time when he tells us what we earned last year."

 BIG IDEA...

What are the key numbers in YOUR business, and how often do you check them?

Our only barometer was the amount of money sat in the bank account. If there was money there, we must be doing ok. We hadn't got a clue how much (if any) of that money was ours though, and how much would have to be paid out to the VAT man, to cover Corporation Tax, PAYE, to pay creditors and future cash flow. Did we have surplus cash to invest, or did we need to borrow money to trade through a lean spell?

No. Bloody. Idea.

Know and OWN your KPIs

Now though, my team produce a monthly key performance indicator (KPI) report which answers all these questions, and more – we've identified almost 100 numbers that we need to monitor constantly, in order to know whether the business is on track to deliver the goals I've set. So I can see how the cost of stock has risen over the last 12 months, match that trend against the gross and net margins, see how that impacts the average customer lifetime value, and use that data to immediately influence how much we're willing to spend to get a new customer.

It also shows us when we need to be delivering value to our existing customers, as several of the numbers that we need to know and monitor on a monthly basis revolve around customer engagement and satisfaction. We can see customer service issues, and resolve them before they become BIG problems – this, in turn, increases the average lifetime value, which again means we can spend more to acquire customers.

Thanks to the KPI report, I can see beyond a shadow of a doubt, that investing in delivering truly amazing customer service results in customers that stay with us longer, who spend more money with us, return more often, and refer more of their friends. And it's no longer just a gut feeling that this is the case – I've got cold, hard facts and figures to back it up.

This is why we work so hard on conversion rate optimisation, and the user experience – whilst all of our competitors are focusing on the top of their funnel, chucking in more and more customers all the time, we're able to use the data that we've got from the KPI reports to spend most of our time working on the middle of the funnel and the bottom of the funnel. This then has the knock-on effect of increasing the value of every single person we add to the top of the funnel, which means that we can afford to spend more on adding new people to the funnel than our competitors.

Often, I'll be chatting to these rivals at a trade show or conference, and they'll ask me how I can still afford to use a particular marketing channel, usually telling me that "they want so much money for a lead these days that it's just not profitable" – and their brain shuts down at that point. Just as Robert Kiyosaki was told by his Rich Dad, "Poor people say 'I can't afford it', the rich say 'HOW can I afford it?'"

Again, financial literacy is the difference.

You're not still doing your own accounts, are you?

There's an old saying that a good accountant will tell you how much you made last year, whilst a great accountant will ask you how much you wanted to make last year.

I've got my own version of that – I believe that a good accountant will tell you how much you made last year, keep you legal in terms of tax, regulations etc., and provide you with quarterly reports, as well as be on hand to answer queries etc., whereas a great accountant will do all of that, plus work with you to plan how much money you'd like the business to make in the forthcoming tax year, set goals to make sure you're on track throughout the year, provide feedback on a monthly basis, proactively advise you of any grants or schemes that you could benefit from, and plan your business set up with your long term personal financial goals in mind. Not quite as punchy as the original saying, granted – but I think I prefer my version.

If you're just starting out, and think that you can save money by not hiring an accountant, and doing your books yourself, then you're only deluding yourself – in most cases, hiring a decent accountant will actually SAVE you more money in unnecessary tax paid than it'll cost you to hire them. And hiring a professional to do a professional job frees up your time to focus on what you're best at – growing your business.

I'm embarrassed to admit it, but I was doing my own bookkeeping for the first thirteen years of running my own businesses.

I thought that "my business is too complex. No bookkeeper will be able to understand it". And yet I HATED doing the books. Every three months, I would put it off until the very last moment, when the accountant was literally screaming for them, and I'd set aside an entire day to go through all the paperwork, printing off invoices, receipts and locating missing transactions – finding all those random people who had sent me a payment for a handful of euros without telling me who they were, or a few hundred dollars but no invoice or receipt.

For that one day, every three months, I turned into the king of procrastination. I'd do ANYTHING to delay actually going through the paperwork. Usually, it would over-run into a second day too. Two whole days out of my business. Two days that I'm doing NOTHING to get and keep customers. Two days that my business shrinks rather than grows.

It wasn't until I sat down with my mentor one afternoon, and he asked me what my plans were for the following week.

"I've got the bloody books to do."

"What? You're doing your own books? Why the bloody hell haven't you got a bookkeeper doing that?"

I explained all the reasons above – my business is too complex etc.

"Bollocks is it. Have you actually ASKED your accountants if they'd do it?"

Erm, no... Not exactly.

So I did.

"Yes, of course we can!" they said.

"Well, why the bloody hell haven't you mentioned this before on any of the previous 57 times I've moaned to you about how much I hate doing the books?" I didn't reply (but wanted to).

"Just to warn you though, it's going to cost around £200 a quarter"

Where do I sign? £800 a year to NEVER have to do the books again, to get an extra seven or eight days per year growing my business rather than buried in paperwork – hell yeah! And of course, they LOVE doing bookkeeping, so what took me two days of reluctant plodding through, they were whizzing through in a couple of hours with a smile on their face – win/win. They do what they love, and I do what I love.

BIG IDEA...

STOP thinking you need to do it all – outsource everything you don't HAVE to be doing, and focus on what you're best at.

Assets versus liabilities

One of the key takeaways from "Rich Dad, Poor Dad" for me was understanding the difference between an asset and a liability. Put simply, an asset puts money in your pocket, and a liability takes money out of your pocket. Every single financial transaction you make is either one, or the other. There's no in between.

But your mindset can change an asset to a liability, or vice versa. The most successful people I've met have a very strong ability to convert liabilities into assets. That £800 I was paying for bookkeeping shows up in the liability column, but then there's a corresponding line in the asset column where I convert the time I WOULD have spent pushing paper around my desk into actual hard revenue – if I can turn those seven or eight days into more than £800 in profit, then hiring a bookkeeper is an asset, not a liability.

Is buying a speedboat an asset? If all you do is burn around in it all summer long, then it takes money OUT of your pocket, and is a liability. If you hire it out to bankers and lawyers and make a profit, then it puts money INTO your pocket and becomes an asset. The "secret" to getting rich is therefore pretty damn simple – get more assets, and reduce your liabilities. Rinse and repeat.

BIG IDEA...

COLLECT assets. Buy them. Build them. Acquire them. Sweat them.

Assets buying assets

So all I do now – my ONLY job, is to build, buy, acquire and sweat assets.

I turn earned income from my businesses into passive income by buying assets.

I buy property that makes a good ROI, and that I think will go up in value.

I acquire businesses that I can "set and forget" for cash flow.

I buy websites that I can improve the conversion rates on.

I work on improving the middle/bottom of the funnel in all our existing businesses.

I set aside time for personal development on a daily basis.

I find new joint venture (JV) partners that I can work with.

I look for competitors I can acquire.

I create new sales letters and marketing copy, to create campaigns that can be used again and again – turning one off "work" into an evergreen asset that we can simply dust off, tweak and deploy time after time.

In the next chapter, I'll walk you through one of the best assets that I've created – a marketing campaign that we've now re-created several times, and which has earned us a significant chunk of change – one that was created from thin air.

Yes, the business already existed (an asset I bought on eBay for £500 back in 2008), and the mailing list was already there (another asset that I've built up), but the only "cost" of my investment in creating this particular asset was time – around three months' total work from inception to cash in the bank.

I then use that money in the bank – the returns from my assets, to buy more assets. Assets buying assets? That's compounding at work, ladies and gentlemen – Warren Buffett would be proud!

What assets do you own?

What assets can you create?

What assets can you improve the cash flow on?

What liabilities could you turn into an asset?

What liabilities could you reduce, or remove altogether?

Shift your mindset, from hard-working self-employed person, to chief asset builder.

Your only job is, therefore, the same as mine – to build, create, acquire, and sweat assets.

THE BEST MARKETING CAMPAIGN WE EVER RAN...

"Doing business without advertising is like winking at a girl in the dark. You know what you are doing, but nobody else does."

Steuart Henderson Britt

I was at a corporate event the other day, and a couple of guys on the table next to me started chatting about their businesses. As always, when people start talking about small businesses, my ears prick up, so I started ear-wigging. Their conversation went something like this:

Dave's mate: "How's business, Dave?"

Dave: "Oh, you know mate. Really slow at the moment. It's the economy isn't it?"

Dave's mate: "Yeah, that's true. Do you do any advertising?"

Dave: "Nah. Tried that once – it doesn't work."

Dave's mate: "Tell me about it. I had an advert in the Herald when I first started out. Complete waste of money."

"Word of mouth" is NOT a marketing channel

I honestly haven't embellished that account in any way – and Dave and his mate aren't the only ones to feel like this. I speak to a lot of small business owners every week, and nine times out of ten, when I ask them what their biggest source of new customers is, I hear the same line...

"Word of mouth".

"Word of mouth" is often code for "I don't do any marketing at all" – people who rely on word of mouth alone, literally do NOTHING to influence how many new customers they get. They're completely in the hands of fate – they have this Kevin Costner Syndrome, where they think "if I build it, they will come" – well, not if they don't even know you exist, they won't!

Recently, there have been several stories in our local newspaper about small, independently-owned cafés and restaurants closing down, with the owners bemoaning the lack of regular trade, blaming the general public for not turning up, the big chains for taking their business, the council for charging business rates that are too high.

They blame everyone but themselves. The business rates are set in stone. If they'd done some research before setting up shop, they'd have known exactly what they needed to pay. It's the big chains' JOB to compete with local restaurants. They're in business to make money. As should you be.

Which leaves the lack of regular trade.

This is the ONE THING that every café owner and restaurateur CAN influence. By doing regular marketing campaigns, both to spread awareness of their café or restaurant to new customers, but also to remind existing customers that you're there, and encourage them to come back more often.

 BIG IDEA...

It's NOT your customer's job to remember to do business with you – it's YOUR job to remind them.

But in every single one of these "sob stories" that I've read in the local rag, it's the first time I've even HEARD of the café or restaurant.

They've NEVER targeted me as a local resident who likes to eat out with ANY marketing. Not once. They've fallen into the Kevin Costner trap of thinking that all they have to do is open the doors, knock out tasty food, and "they will come".

Well, as these people are finding out the hard way – no, they bloody well won't. "They" don't even know you exist!

If "word of mouth" is your biggest source of new customers, then you're in trouble. Sure, you might be getting by right now, but you're not in control of the flow of new customers – so how can you plan staffing levels, investment in new technology, the growth of the business, when you're not in control of how many people come through your door?

Proper marketing puts you in control of the flow of new customers

For our sports betting business, we run lots of evergreen marketing campaigns to bring in a steady stream of new customers every single day of the week. If you search for certain keywords on Google, or have demonstrated a particular interest on Facebook, there's a bloody good chance you're going to see one of our highly targeted ads.

BIG IDEA...

"Evergreen" marketing campaigns give you a steady STREAM of regular new and returning customers.

That's our bread and butter, and that puts US in control of the flow of new customers.

We also run several big marketing campaigns, which usually last two to three weeks. Sometimes these are designed to bring in new customers (in the four weeks immediately before the Cheltenham Festival in March each year, we bring in nearly 20,000 new customers in our big lead generation campaign), but more often than not, they're sales campaigns.

We ran one such campaign in October 2016, and at the time of writing, it was by far the best campaign we'd ever run in terms of return on investment (ROI). Everything just seemed to fall into place with this campaign – the stars aligned, and we totally smashed it out of the park. It worked so well, that in the immediate aftermath, we decided to fully document the debrief, and use this campaign as the template for ALL future campaigns.

 BIG IDEA...

Big, one-off sales campaigns are designed to do ONE THING – get the tills ringing.

Here's that template...

1. Proper planning

Prevents piss-poor performance. Plan out the entire campaign on paper first. Write all of the copy. Look for holes. Fix leaks. What's missing?

We planned this campaign three months in advance. We identified some potential leaks (places where people might abandon the sales process) with our registration forms, so spent weeks getting our web dev guys to completely overhaul the process, and rewrite everything from scratch. This was hard work, but it was worth the wait, and it was worth the investment – making that change improved our sales conversion rate by over 50%, resulting in literally hundreds of sales, totalling tens of thousands of pounds, that we otherwise just wouldn't have made.

When planning our Cheltenham lead generation campaign every year, we enter everything into a calendar, so the whole team can see the full schedule of what's happening, and when. There are a lot of moving parts in this campaign, with various landing pages going live at different times, more than 30 different emails that need writing and scheduling, live Facebook videos that need planning in advance, a 32-page magazine that needs writing, printing and delivering, around 40 affiliate partners who need liaising with to agree commission structures and provide with copy, and updated Facebook and Google Adwords spends.

You can't just rock up and go straight into a full-blown marketing campaign, hoping to wing it. You've got to know what the objective is, and how you're going to meet that objective.

BIG IDEA...

Fail to prepare, prepare to fail...

2. Reason for the campaign?

It's my dog's birthday. My kid learned to walk. We've got a new product. We've moved into a new office. We were featured on the TV. It's National Donut Day. The reason itself doesn't matter – you've just got to HAVE one.

For this campaign, it was the third anniversary of a product that we sell. Literally, "We launched this product three years ago this month" – pretty weak as far as reasons go, but by attaching the "third birthday" story to the campaign, people were able to make an emotional connection to the campaign.

3. Go overboard on value, don't just discount

10% discount is not an offer. Let me just repeat that a second...

10% DISCOUNT IS NOT AN OFFER.

BIG IDEA...

Pricing is NOT your only weapon in the marketing battle. SAVE your price cuts for a last resort.

If you're putting a campaign together and are thinking about having a 10% discount as your hook, then please, I implore you – stop! No-one actually values a 10% discount – it's the same crap, bland, vanilla "discount" that everyone else offers. It isn't persuasive enough to get enough people taking action, and that entire 10% discount comes straight out of YOUR margin, which could reduce your net profit margin by as much as 30%!

Rather than discounting the price, try adding value to what you're selling. We heavily discounted the first month on our campaign, but after that, it was full price all the way. What we also did was add things that people who bought the product outside of the campaign didn't get – mugs, tickets to racing, private access to our tipster etc. Ideally, you want to make the offer so damn good that it's a total no-brainer. You've reversed the risk, so that from the customer's point of view, they're not going to lose even if the product is rubbish (which of course it isn't... is it??). For our campaign, the customer's risk was just £3 – if the product did what we said it would, they'd have won a few hundred quid, got a free mug and a ticket to the Gold Cup. If it didn't work out, they could still keep the mug, and they'd only "lost" £3.

No. Brainer.

 BIG IDEA...

What can you do to REVERSE the risk in your customer's eyes?

---

4. Multiple deadlines

Deadlines get people to take ACTION. When do you think HMRC's busiest day of the year is? Yep, it's January 31st – deadline day for everyone to pay their self-assessment tax. When are most football transfers completed? Yep, you've guessed it – transfer deadline day.

So, you've GOT to have a deadline in your marketing campaign. But why stop at one?

BIG IDEA...

There's NOTHING like a deadline to get people to take action.

In our campaign, we had FOUR separate deadlines:

- The first 50 people to buy got a free mug
- Buy before Wednesday lunchtime, and get entered into a draw to win a "money can't buy" prize
- This special offer will be withdrawn at 5pm on Monday 31st October
- Once you've bought, stay with us until February 14th, and we'll take you on a VIP trip to the races

This gives people the incentive to act NOW, regardless of what stage they are at in the buying journey. Those that are ready to buy from day one get the absolute best deal.

Those that missed the best deal and are kicking themselves for missing out get the next best deal. And those that wait until the very last minute to do anything (a.k.a the vast majority of people) still get the offer. But then we also reward loyalty by giving them an incentive to stay with us long-term (which means they are more committed to the product and become better customers!)

If you were to analyse our sales numbers for this campaign, you'd see massive spikes on each of these deadlines. Sure, we make sales every time we send an email, but send an email on deadline day, and you get LOTS of sales. No-one wants to miss out.

5. Follow up – LOTS

As I said, we make sales every time we send an email out. So how many emails should you send during a sales campaign? Two? Three? Whatever number you're thinking of right now, I'd probably say treble it! Double it at least... We sent eight emails in this campaign, over a 16-day campaign. And EVERY campaign we do has a minimum of seven.

That's one to introduce the offer, and six to follow up and close sales. Every single one of them makes sales. Don't fall into the trap of saying the same thing seven times though. Each email should do ONE (ideally just one, but certainly no more than two) of the following things:

- Introduce an offer
- Introduce a deadline
- Remind of a deadline
- Offer social proof
- Counter objections
- Give a rational reason to buy
- Give an emotional reason to buy
- Get the reader to like and trust you

And on top of that, there's one more thing that you HAVE to do in every email...

ASK FOR THE SALE!

You'd be amazed how many sales emails I see from people who don't even ask people for the sale. "Get in touch if you'd like more info" is NOT asking for the sale – "Click here to grab one of the first 50 places" is asking for the sale.

Just keep following up – "Till they buy, or till they die" as the old sales mantra goes.

 BIG IDEA...

The fortune's in the follow up.

6. Counter objections and offer social proof

This is what to fill all those emails, direct mail, leaflets and web pages with – literally flood your marketing with testimonials (include a photo if possible, even better get video testimonials!), stats, case studies and stories, to showcase real people having real success using your service/product.

People won't believe what you tell them – after all, you're a marketer who's out to sell them something – but they will believe your customers when THEY tell them. So use your existing clients to counter objections ("I know they're not the cheapest, but they've been worth every penny"), and re-enforce why they need your product, and why they should take action right now.

This was the secret sauce that made all the difference in our campaign. We were selling a horse racing tipping service, and the weekend before the "end of offer" deadline, our tipster hit a BIG win, meaning that our members won hundreds (and in some cases thousands!) of pounds in one day. Without being prompted, our Facebook feed was suddenly flooded with people posting up their winning betslips, showing off their winnings, and telling us (and crucially, the thousands of people who HADN'T yet subscribed) how great the service was.

BIG IDEA...

ALWAYS collect testimonials, and use the best ones in your marketing.

Imagine that you're one of our prospects. You'd have had by this point, around four or five of our emails, maybe one piece of direct mail, and seen a few live videos on Facebook. You're AWARE of the offer, but you haven't signed up for whatever reason. And then you see this post from one of your friends:

"OMG! Only joined last week. Got my free mug in the post this morning, and won £855 this afternoon – not bad for £3!"

How would you feel? And how quickly would you be reaching for your credit card?

That's the power of social proof.

7. Multiple Media – Online / Offline

Send an email. Then call. Text. Post on Facebook, Twitter, and Snapchat. Send them a WhatsApp message. Send them some direct mail. Call again. Go and knock on their door. Shake their hand, look them in the eyes, and ask for the sale.

Do you know who one of the biggest senders of direct mail is in the UK?

Google.

A dotcom company... one that works online – a technology giant, using stamps and letters! Why is that?

Because it works.

Think back to the early 2000s – your letterbox was full of junk mail, and you got all excited when you received an email. Nowadays it's the other way around – your email inbox is full of junk, and you get excited when you get a letter in the post (that isn't a bank statement or a letter from HMRC!).

We usually try and include at least one piece of direct mail in every campaign we do – this ensures we stand out, as not one of our competitors does this. We stand head and shoulders above them in people's expectations, therefore.

We also make use of another "traditional" form of sales – we pick up the phone and actually speak to people – revolutionary, I tell you!

But it's amazing how often our telesales team hear the line "It's so nice to speak to a real person these days" or "It's reassuring to know there's a real person behind this website" – and you'll soon find out what objections they've got, and why they haven't bought yet – which you can incorporate into the rest of your copy, to close more people!

BIG IDEA...

Don't be afraid to pick up the PHONE and call your customers.

8. Follow up MORE

Come on, admit it – you chickened out last time, didn't you? How many times did you follow up? Once? Twice? Get back on the phone now. Send another email now. Till they buy, or till they die, remember?

Are you afraid of upsetting someone, or worried that a few people might unsubscribe? Good.

You WANT people to moan that you're emailing them too much.

You WANT some of them to unsubscribe.

That's how you purge your list of the people who have no intention of buying stuff from you, and who aren't a good fit for you. If people aren't moaning about the number of emails, you're not sending enough.

If your product or service can genuinely improve their lives or their businesses, and you can genuinely help them in some way, then it is your duty and responsibility to make sure that they buy your product or service. If you didn't do EVERYTHING in your power to convince them, then you will have failed them, and you will have failed yourself.

You don't want to fail, do you?

Good.

Till they buy.

Or till they die.

 BIG IDEA...

Follow up "TILL THEY BUY, OR TILL THEY DIE..."

---

9. Next time?

Did this campaign work? Awesome! When are you going to repeat it, then? Don't leave a great sales campaign to wither and die – dust it off every six months, or every 12 months and repeat it.

Even better, perform a debrief after each campaign – what worked? What didn't? Which elements can be improved upon? What objections did you fail to overcome? What media worked best? Can you fit another follow-up in?

Put simply, what would you do differently next time?

Once you have the answer to that question – document exactly what you would do next time. And then schedule it in so that it HAPPENS next time, and doesn't end up being forgotten whilst you're lost in the day-to-day.

DO YOU WANT TO BUILD A SNOWMAN?

"Compound interest is the 8th wonder of the world. He who understands it, earns it... he who doesn't – pays it!"

Albert Einstein

Warren Buffett is my business hero. Always has been, and always will be. He's the fourth-richest man on the planet, a self-made billionaire ($67bn at last count) who intends to give 99% of it away, and who sees himself as a down to earth "Cherry Coke and cheeseburger guy" when he could afford to chow down on caviar and champagne on a daily basis.

For me though, the best thing about Warren Buffett is the lessons that we can learn from him. And lesson number one is the power of compounding.

 BIG IDEA...

Be more Warren! Check out his HBO documentary "Becoming Warren Buffett" for an insight into his genius.

Start building your snowball

Imagine you're standing at the top of a huge hill. It's snowing, and these wonderful large snowflakes are gently floating to the ground and laying all around you. You hold out your hand and one lands in your palm. You hold your hand there for a few moments and you get a collection of snowflakes there, and then gently close your hand to make a tiny ball of snow. As the snowflakes keep coming down, you just keep packing them on to make your snowball bigger and bigger, until eventually, it's the size of a tennis ball. Then you lay your snowball on the snow-covered ground at the top of this hill, and gently start rolling. The hill will do all the work. By the time your snowball has rolled down the hill, it'll be bigger than your house – and it all started with just a few individual flakes and a big hill.

In compounding terms, the snowflakes are pound coins, and the hill represents time. Most people think of compounding as simply "interest on your interest". Buffett thinks of it in terms of the effect that the "hill of time" can have on your cash.

When he met the first Mrs Buffett and was persuaded that it was time to settle down and get married, he was mortified to learn that she wanted to buy a house. She didn't see a problem – he'd already made his first million dollars by this point. And the house was going to cost just $57,000.

To Warren Buffett though, $57,000 was just what it was worth at that moment in time (at the top of the hill). In his mind, $57,000 compounded for 20 years at 20% was $2 million after he'd rolled that $57k snowball down the hill. He said "If I spend $57,000 today on that house, it will actually cost me two million dollars. Why the hell am I going to spend two million dollars on a house?"

 BIG IDEA...

Where you are RIGHT NOW is the compound effect of your life so far.

I'm sure most men reading this will understand who won that argument though – Warren still lives in that same $57,000 house even though he's now one of the richest men on the planet (but I'll bet you anything he still grumbles every time the Forbes rich list comes out that he'd have an extra hundred million or two if only he hadn't bought that damn house back in the fifties!)

The "guaranteed winner" fruit machine

Compounding is a tactic that I've used in almost all of my businesses over the last 16 years.

From the very first one that I started with £100 and sold for £120,000, to the one I bought for £6.5k, and made over half a million from over the subsequent three years, to the one I bought for £500 on eBay in 2008, and still own to this day, which now turns over £700k a year and employs six full time members of staff.

I didn't take a penny out of any of those businesses for at least 18 months. Every single penny they earned was reinvested in them in the form of increased advertising and marketing spends, better design, SEO, staff, systems, conversion rate optimisation, PR campaigns and bringing in experts (but mainly increased advertising and marketing spend – we really ramped those up once the business model was proven!).

 BIG IDEA...

The easiest way to compound is to REINVEST profits BEFORE paying yourself more money (especially in the early years)...

The one I'm most proud of is probably that very first business – I turned £100 to into an annual revenue stream of several hundred thousand, over the course of a couple of years, despite having no business experience whatsoever. I was still working in the day job for the first 18 months – whilst reinvesting everything that the business earned.

When I could afford it, I got a domain name, then hired a web designer to do me a logo. As the revenue grew, I got better hosting, better design, some newsletter software. Eventually, I had enough money to go to London and attend a conference and networking event.

It took me nine months to earn my first cheque. I wish I'd framed it now rather than cashing it in, as it was only for £13.51. But it was really symbolic because the day I got that cheque, I knew that I could make a success of it, and sure enough, just nine months later, I gave up the day job.

That meant I could compound even more time, as I could now work more hours per week entirely focused on my business. So I learnt how to generate more traffic, how to write copy to convert that traffic into sales, and saw my business grow and grow. I was able to jump on Google Adwords literally the day it launched in the UK, and buy traffic for one cent per click – traffic that was worth ten times that to me.

It was like a fruit machine that chucked out ten times what you put in – and I compounded that over several months until eventually, just two years after getting that first cheque for £13.51, I was pulling in £20,000 to £30,000 some months, with the only overheads being my ad spend. That gravy train didn't last long, but just that short period of rolling the snowball down a 12 month hill, at something crazy like 3,000% annual ROI set me up for the rest of my career.

So I'm now emulating the mighty "Oracle of Omaha" in my own businesses – the last two businesses I've launched have a 20-year compounding strategy, whereby we're planning to reinvest every penny for the next two decades, and just pack on the snow, and roll it down the hill. If we can put £100k of our money into a business, and compound it by just 10% a year, we'll have nearly £700k after two decades. If we can grow it by 20% a year, we're talking £3.8m, and an average 30% annual growth rate would see us turn that £100k into just over £19m.

Now, a 30% annual return sounds really high when you compare it with the 0.25% which is the best you'll get from a high street current account at the time of writing, but it's actually really conservative when you look at some of the ROIs we can get from our marketing spend, where 500% or 600% ROIs are entirely normal, and 1,000%+ isn't out of the question. That's why I prefer to invest in businesses and property rather than ISAs or Premium Bonds!

BIG IDEA...

Investing in your business can give you MUCH bigger returns than almost any other investment product.

At the time of writing this book, the "official" rate of inflation (the amount that the government says prices of "an average basket of goods" rise each year) is at a two-year high of 1.2%. You'll note my use of "official" in the previous sentence, as I believe this to be complete and utter BS. The Office for National Statistics has been fudging the figures for years, removing items that went up in price too much, and replacing them with cheaper items to keep the "official" figure nice and low.

Chocolate bars haven't gone up in price that much over the last five years, but they have shrunk in size by around 35%, which makes them a lot more than 1.2% per year more expensive. My energy bills have doubled in the last decade.

How does that equate to 1.2%?

And that's before you get me started on the quantitative easing (i.e. printing new money) that successive governments have embarked on as a way of kicking the can of insurmountable national debt down the road for the next parliament to worry about. The more money that's in circulation, the less each pound is worth – it's a simple supply and demand equation.

I would say the true rate of inflation is more like 5% to 10% per annum. Put simply, that means if you're earning less than 5% returns per year on your money, then your wealth is actually reducing in real terms (i.e. not how much money you have, but what you can buy with it!).

The ultimate pension plan

If you're sat on a big snowball of cash and are rolling it down a nice "safe" ISA hill, and you're getting maybe 1.25% if you're lucky, then after inflation you're still getting poorer and poorer every year, and it's time to start looking for a different hill. One that may not be "risk free", and certainly won't be 100% passive, but that has the potential to pay a much better return than you'll get anywhere on the high street.

BIG IDEA...

Do business like an investor. Invest like a businessman.

You can teach yourself how to grow a business (hint: reading books like this helps...)

You can learn how to trade Forex or the stock market. These are not without risks, but then "zero risk" is for the uneducated – educate yourself, find out what you need to do to make these sort of returns, and then start making some calculated risks.

But what if you don't have a big snowball to begin with?

Well, If you could put aside £100 to £150 a month, and compound that at just 10% per year, after 20 years you'd have somewhere between £75k and £100k to play with!

A few weeks back, I spent two whole days in one of my businesses trying to shave £150 a month off our overheads. After an hour or so, I nearly gave up – "my time is worth more than £150" I thought.

BIG IDEA...

It doesn't always "take money to make money". You can make money with TIME, thanks to compounding.

But then the metaphorical voice of Warren Buffett gave me a scolding and reminded me that £150 was just what it's worth TODAY. £150 a month shaved off our overheads and placed into our investment fund instead, and compounded at 10% turns into £108,598 after twenty years. I think £108k for two days work is actually pretty damn good!

£250 a month, compounded at 10% for 40 years? £1.4 million. £300 a month, at 15% over the same timeframe? £6.9 million!

How do you turn £300 into £6.9 million? Delayed gratification. Rather than spending that £300 NOW on a monthly car payment, forego that shiny new Beemer, and commit that £300 to investing in your business, or investment portfolio instead.

You can always get the car once your business is throwing off excess cash left, right and centre – but by delaying the gratification of getting a fancy new set of wheels, you can ensure that your long-term wealth creation is taken care of first.

As they tell you during a pre-flight safety briefing – "always fit your own oxygen mask before helping others", so it is with wealth creation – always make sure your "Get Rich Slowly" plan is in place before spending money on things like cars, houses and holidays that make you APPEAR rich.

 BIG IDEA...

How do you turn £300 into £6.9 million?
DELAYED GRATIFICATION.

If you can start early enough, compounding can take care of your retirement, making sure you don't have to take part in the usual 40/40/40 retirement plan that most people sign up to (where you spend 40 years working 40 hours a week, to then try and live on 40% of your income when you retire).

Start early enough and do reasonably well (say 10% per year) – and for around £200 a month, most people could become a millionaire in their lifetime.

If you want to lose the next few hours of your life, Google "compound interest calculator" and play with some figures.

Or better yet, get out there, and start building that damn snowball...

MULTIPLE STREAMS OF INCOME...

"Never rely on a single source of income. Make investments to create a second source. You don't want to test the depth of the river with both your feet."

Warren Buffett

Ah, "multiple streams of income" – the classic war cry of MLM spammers the world over. But unlike their pyramid-shaped business model, and "annoy all your friends until you've got none left" way of selling, they might actually have a point here.

What happens when your stream runs dry?

Remember Robert Kiyosaki and his two dads?

One of the standout lessons for me from Kiyosaki's tale is that his "Rich Dad" has all sorts of different businesses.

He owns real estate all over Hawaii and several major investments. He owned supermarkets, cafés, and restaurants, and invested in stocks, gilts, and bonds. In other words, he has those mythical "multiple streams of income" (MSIs) in abundance.

But what's the benefit of having multiple streams of income?

The main one is security. If you've only got one single revenue stream, and that stream dries up – it's game over for you. Just in the same way that I used to have one single marketing pillar (SEO) pre-2012, when that pillar dried up, so did the customers, and so did the money.

I managed to dodge that bullet by very quickly changing my model to add second, third and fourth pillars (email list, Facebook, and Twitter). But others weren't so lucky.

One of our rivals relied almost entirely on a single stream of income from a single source – affiliate commissions from a UK bookmaker called Blue Square.

Over the previous seven years or so, they'd built this revenue stream up to a decent level, whereby they were making a healthy £300k a year profit from this stream.

BIG IDEA...

Relying on ONE revenue stream, ONE marketing pillar, ONE customer, or ONE product is asking for trouble.

And then, in December 2012, Blue Square was acquired by Betfair, who sent an email out, effectively shutting down the Blue Square brand, and nullifying the affiliate deals with immediate effect – from getting a cheque for £25k every month, to "game over", just like that.

That served as a real wake-up call for me, and so I worked hard over the next 12 months to build additional revenue streams into ALL my businesses – we added paid membership options, introduced new continuity products, spread our affiliate risk across more partners – everything we could possibly do to avoid a "Blue Square situation".

When you've got one single type of revenue stream, and when 80% of your revenue in that stream comes from one source, you're at massive risk of failure.

That's pretty much the situation we were in around the start of 2013.

As I write this, just over four years later, that same business now has seven different types of revenue stream, and the one partner which made up 80% of our income now "just" accounts for 35% of our income – still high enough that we'd worry if we lost it, but low enough that it wouldn't be game over for us if we did – we would survive.

Create new products to generate multiple streams of income from your existing customers

A good place to look for ways to create more income streams is to ask your customers what they want. For years, a small number of our members had been telling us that they didn't want to work with our affiliate partners. In the past, we'd turned them away!

So we created a small £4.95 per month product that was only offered to those people. It sold – in the hundreds.

Then we trawled through the most frequently raised topics from the customer service logs. Loads of people had been asking for us to send them tips via SMS text message. Hey presto! We created another paid product – SMS Club at £8.95 per month. Again, we sold hundreds of those.

So we kept on looking at what our members were asking us for – and we delivered. A dedicated "Lucky 15" service (a type of bet that can win big money from small stakes); a magazine; a horse racing syndicate; horse ratings; direct access to our tipster; days at the races.

We simply asked our community what they wanted, and then gave it to them. It was no surprise that they bought what we launched, as we knew in advance that there was a demand for it.

 BIG IDEA...

Take the risk out of developing new revenue streams by crowd-sourcing your next product. ASK your customers what they want to buy from you.

We were then also in a position to be able to buy up some "rival" websites – for the smaller ones, we simply closed them down and redirected the traffic to our main brand.

One or two of the larger sites we kept on, running them as their own brand, or where they were complimentary to the main site rather than competing, we brought them into the fold as a "sister site", and cross-promoted them – providing yet another stream of income.

Wherever possible, I like to create residual income streams. This is where you get paid every month or every week, but only have to make the sale once.

This is why I like creating and buying membership websites, as well as commercial and residential property. If I sign up a member to our £77 a month One Percent Club mentoring group, I'm going to get paid £77 every single month that they remain a member. Get 100 people in that group, and I've got a residual income stream of £92,400 a year.

With residual income streams like that, I start the month knowing roughly what sort of cash is going to flow into my business. I'm not starting on £0 and having to go out and sell in order to meet payroll or to pay the bills.

Residual income gives you the freedom to go out and create more residual income streams, knowing that the bills will be paid no matter how many sales you make – it removes that financial pressure that causes many small business owners to make bad decisions because they "need the money".

BIG IDEA...

Residual income removes the "FEAST and FAMINE" peaks and troughs of cash flow that a lot of small businesses suffer, and allows you to focus entirely on getting and keeping new customers.

Eggs is eggs?

More and more businesses are moving towards this residual, membership, subscription-style model. Take Naked Wines for example – rather than buying a bottle of wine whenever you feel like it, you pay them a monthly subscription, and every now and then they'll email you telling you what wines you might like, and they send it to you. You've paid upfront – but you haven't missed it because they drip it out monthly.

Given the "buy when you want what we're selling" model, Naked Wines might average £100 a year from the typical customer. On the subscription model, they take an average of £240 a year!

If you're a gardener, stop charging people "per job", and get them on a monthly Direct Debit, that pays you every month – even through the winter. The customers will feel they're getting a bargain in the summer when you're there every week, and you get paid through the lean winter months when nothing grows.

Are you an MOT / servicing garage?

Stop charging people hundreds of pounds in one hit every year for their MOT and service – get them on a £19 a month plan that includes their MOT, service, and discounted prices on any other work they have done. When they need to spend an extra £200 getting it through the MOT, they'll be happier spending that than they would have been if you had hit them with the full £400+ bill in one go. Throw in a few "extras" like washing their car for free every time it's in for a service, and you'll be a massive hit with the punters.

 BIG IDEA...

What do YOU do that you could charge a monthly subscription for?

We work with a local farm which sells eggs. They pay decent money to attend the local "good food" markets and line up alongside all the other traders.

Strolling past the stalls, you see the same thing time and time again – small business owners paying their fees, to sell their wares once to the general public.

Then, four weeks later, they do it again.

They make one sale. They don't capture that customer's details, they don't sell anything to them for weeks on end, and even then, in order to make the sale next time, it's up to the customer to remember to attend the market, and choose to buy again.

Not so with our eggs man. We managed to get him to understand the power of the subscription model. He's not the only person at the market selling free range eggs. In fact, most of the time, he isn't even selling ANY eggs.

He's selling SUBSCRIPTIONS to his egg delivery service.

Every Sunday morning, without fail, I wake up to two dozen eggs on my front doorstep. I pay £19.93 a month via Direct Debit, and I've got twenty-four freshly laid, free-range eggs delivered from the farm to my door every single week without fail.

His competitors are going around flogging their eggs one dozen at a time. He's realised that a subscription customer is worth considerably more than a dozen eggs – if the average customer stays for a few years and takes two dozen eggs a week, they're worth more than £500 (in their lifetime). So he stopped selling £2.30 eggs and started selling £500 subscriptions.

 BIG IDEA...
Are you selling £2.30 eggs or £500 subscriptions?

Just changing his thinking like this has transformed his business. He knows now that just ONE new subscription customer per market more than pays for the investment in the long term. And with a low price point for a great product, he normally walks away with five or six new subscribers from every market he goes to.

With the pressure to meet cash flow removed, he's free to focus on getting new customers, but also putting things in place to keep more customers.

He knows that if he can increase the average amount of time a subscription customer stays with him by six months, that makes EVERY customer worth another £120.

BIG IDEA...

With a subscription model, you can focus more on KEEPING customers by wowing them.

Eggs is eggs. But you can sell a dozen eggs for £2.30, or you can sell a few hundred dozen for £500+, and the effort is much the same.

Which would you prefer?

I opened this chapter with a quote from my business hero Warren Buffett, talking about making investments to create a second source of income.

And that's actually the main objective of my businesses right now – to create investments that will provide a significant income for my "retirement" (I don't plan on ever ACTUALLY retiring – I tried it once when I was 27, but it'd be nice to have the choice!) in a couple of decades' time, and to provide for my descendants for generations to come.

What business are you in?

Ray Kroc, of McDonald's fame, was a guest speaker at Harvard Business School back in the 1970s, at the height of the burger restaurant's expansion all across America, and he stuck around after the lecture to have lunch with some of the students. The conversation inevitably turned to the quality of the food they were eating, compared to the quality of a McDonald's burger.

Kroc didn't miss a beat. "What business am I in folks?" he asked.

There then followed an awkward silence as the students wondered if they'd really heard the question correctly. "Come on, seriously. What business am I in?"

Eventually, one student felt brave enough to take the bait – "Well Ray, surely everyone in America knows you're in the burger business!"

"Wrong," said Kroc, "I'm in the real estate business."

"McDonald's sells burgers so that it can buy the land that every one of our restaurants sits on. Sure, we make money from selling burgers. But the real wealth comes from owning the land."

McDonald's now has more than 65,000 restaurants worldwide – and they own the land underneath every one of them. They're the world's largest owner of real estate, with prime locations in just about every major city, in every country. Oh, and they still sell burgers.

I now think in a similar way – I'm not in the sports betting business, nor am I in the marketing business. I'm not even in the property business. I'm in the investment business. My job is to build investments – for my future, and for future generations. Sure, I achieve that by selling sports betting tips, working with small business owners on their marketing, and buying and developing property.

 BIG IDEA...

What business are you REALLY in?

But the focus – the end goal – is the investment pot. That "second stream of income" that Warren Buffett talked about.

- Stream #1 – income from my various businesses (which have MSI themselves).

- Stream #2 – income from my investments (which again, have their own MSI)

The profits from the businesses (Stream #1) either get compounded back into other businesses or diverted to Stream #2 to create investments.

The MSI snowball

We sold our freebie website "net free stuff" in 2007. We took the profits from that and piled them into a mobile phone insurance business, a live sports streaming company, a travel website. Then we took the profits from those and created the huge sports betting brands. Once they were up and running, we bought up a few competitors and we grew exponentially.

Once that was bringing in some significant profits, we then looked towards property and started buying up flats and houses in the North of England – from one bedroom flats in Bradford city centre, to redeveloping an old warehouse in Cheshire. We've bought burial plots in London, and invested in a flotation spa in Norwich, and a five-star hotel in Wales.

This has all been to create multiple streams of investment income. This book? Another stream of income.

I've done the same outside the business too, personally investing in animation art, silver bullion, stocks, shares, and Forex trading. I've got professionals looking after hedge funds and pensions for me, and I've even got a "professional gambling fund" that backs our horse racing tips as a methodical investment!

These types of investment are not for everyone. You need to educate yourself financially to quite a high level, and be willing to accept some risks (and potential loss of investments) – but I'm comfortable that I've spread the risk accordingly. It's all well and good chasing 20% average annual returns, but I'd also like to be able to sleep at night without worrying about my portfolio.

One thing you do need to be careful of though – don't spread your risk so much that you actually end up having loads of tiny trickling puddles rather than nice fast-flowing streams. Using the 80/20 principle, there will always be one or two revenue streams that far outweigh all the others combined. Neglect these at your peril.

You should spend the majority of your time looking after your main income source, and then spend a SMALL amount of time hunting for and creating new revenue streams. Don't ALWAYS be chasing the shiny new object!

As always, no-one puts it better than Warren Buffett though, so let's finish the chapter as we started it, with a quote from the Oracle of Omaha...

"They say you shouldn't put all your eggs in one basket. I say put MOST of your eggs in one basket, and watch that basket like a hawk."

Warren Buffett

MAGIC INGREDIENT #4 – ENVIRONMENT
(A.K.A. BE CAREFUL WHO YOU LISTEN TO...)

"Why is he wasting his time and money on this internet thing?"

My mother-in-law

I'm into juicing

No, not the type where you inject yourself with anabolic steroids to get "He-Man" size muscles in a couple of weeks – the one where you drink broccoli and celery for breakfast. Granted, that doesn't sound very appealing, but it's been a life changer for me – just changing this one habit resulted in me losing around two stone in weight, having more energy, better sleep, healthier skin, nails, hair. I hardly ever get ill anymore, and just seem to function much, much better as a result.

This is why I got so irate when I was dicking around on Facebook (yes, even I am guilty of this!), and saw that one of my friends had posted how happy she was to have done a few days of a "juice cleanse" – how much better she was feeling, how much more energy, blah, blah, blah. You get the message. But it wasn't her post that got my back up, it was a comment from one of her well-meaning "friends", who said:

"I watched a TV documentary once about juicing. They said that when you juice fruits and vegetables – you saturate your ability to absorb free radicals – you get too many in too short a time, it's like a sugar rush. Your body will end up absorbing less for long periods of time. When you EAT fruit and vegetables – your body has to work to get them out and they are absorbed steadily over time. These results were measured in the lab. My opinion is – eat well, avoid the juicers."

Well, he certainly makes a compelling case, doesn't he? But who should you listen to? Your friend who watched a documentary on TV once? Or the person who's done it for years and can speak from real experience?

But surely, the documentary makers are the experts? After all, it was measured "in the lab"! I've watched hundreds of documentaries about everything from the Iraq War to the future of education, and one thing always leaps out at me – every documentary maker has an opinion, an agenda. They have a point of view, and they want to "open your eyes" to that point of view in 45 minutes of TV.

But they're only human.

We all want to push our opinions and points of view onto others.

I believe juicing could save hundreds and thousands of lives every year and save the NHS billions in the long run, but that's just my opinion. It's up to you to decide whether you want to listen to me or not.

What you put in your mouth affects your health. What you put in your head affects your wealth.

Just because you have a microphone doesn't mean everyone should listen

One thing I advise anyone to do is to check out the credentials of anyone they're considering taking advice from. I was listening to a podcast recently, all about building wealth through investment. Just the sort of topic I love to listen to!

But it wasn't long before alarm bells started ringing.

During an episode on property investment, the presenter spent a few minutes detailing why property was such a fantastic investment vehicle (I've got a couple of property companies, so this wasn't news to me!), and why everyone should have some property in their portfolio. So far, so standard.

Until he dropped the bombshell.

"Of course, I don't own any investment property just yet, but I hope to one day."

What? You've just spent twenty minutes telling me I should be doing something, that you as the so-called "expert" don't do yourself?

 BIG IDEA...

Ensure those you take advice from are QUALIFIED to be giving it.

If you HAVE built wealth and you say that property is a good tool for building wealth, why the hell don't you own any? It wasn't long before more and more alarm bells were ringing for me either – he'd introduce one guest with the line "Of course, I'm not as rich as him" and another with "I haven't got his money", and by the time I'd listened to about three or four episodes, I had this guy pigeon-holed.

He's an IFA.

He's just a financial advisor with a microphone.

He spends his days selling life insurance and ISAs to people and maybe plays a little in the stock market. He's certainly not an investor, definitely not building significant wealth, and 100% NOT someone I should be listening to, at this stage in my career.

If I'm the John of twenty years ago, who's still a civil servant working for 15 grand a year, then yes – I want to know about which is the best ISA to invest in, how to get more out of my pension, how to try and prepare for a retirement that I'm not going to be able to afford. But as a business owner who actually has got serious ambition to grow my investment portfolio and to actually become seriously wealthy, no, he's not the guy to listen to.

The guy that I need to listen to, is someone like Grant Cardone, who's built up a $500m real estate empire in the US. I may not have ambitions anywhere near that high, but this guy's been there and done exactly what I want to do (and then some!). He's gone from where I am now, to where I want to be. He didn't want to stop there, but I can get off the ride whenever I want to.

When he talks, I listen.

If I'm looking to build serious wealth in property, who am I going to listen to? Am I going to listen to the IFA with a microphone, that doesn't invest in property even though he knows it's a good idea to, or am I going to listen to the guy who's got half a BILLION dollars' worth of bloody real estate?

One of my mentors used to say to me "Free advice is worth every penny" – and that's why I prefer to listen to people who charge for their advice now.

I've had no end of business advice from people who've never owned a business, and investment advice from people who think "investing" is looking around for a good savings account.

Whose advice are YOU most likely to listen to?

 BIG IDEA...

Free advice is worth every penny.

If you're like most people, it's likely to be the handful of people that you spend the most time with, your immediate network of peers. We've all heard it said that "you are the sum of the five people closest to you", or "your network is your net worth". Well, this is one cliché that is true. That immediate environment around you sculpts who you are.

Hang around with five drug-addicts, you're likely to become the sixth. Five thieves? Chances are you'll become thief #6.

This works both ways though – your best chance of becoming a millionaire is to hang around with five millionaires – their habits, routines, ways of thinking, ability to spot an opportunity, the language they use, the networks they have access to.

This will all rub off on you via osmosis, and before you know it, you're millionaire number six.

Plan on making it REALLY big? – Check out the Forbes Rich List, and make friends with five of those people!

Choose your friends VERY carefully

If there's ONE lesson that I could travel back in time, and impart to the 19-year-old version of myself, it would be that who you hang around with is crucial – it can make or break you. And the five people I was hanging around with the most back in 1997 were infinitely more likely to break me than to be the making of me.

 BIG IDEA...

Who you hang around with REALLY matters.

They were all typical nineties "lads" – blokes who liked nothing more than watching football, going out and getting blind drunk every night (yes, I mean EVERY night), and sleeping with as many women as possible.

This meant that I watched football, got blind drunk (almost) every night, and... well you get the picture.

There were just two small problems with that lifestyle for me – first of all, I was engaged to be married, and secondly, I was trying to build a career within the civil service.

Having a few beers on a Friday night with your mates is great fun. Having 10 pints on a Tuesday night, and then having to get up at 7am on a Wednesday morning for a team meeting (when you only rolled in the door at 2am, having somehow got home – I have literally no idea how I made it home some nights!) isn't.

And fiancées don't stick around long after months and months of neglect, turning down romantic nights in with a movie and takeaways in favour of going out with your mates, drinking till you fall over, and trying to get off with anything with a pulse.

So I lost my fiancée – the love of my life, the woman I was going to spend the rest of my life with.

(Don't cry too hard for me though – I found a better one once I'd sorted my life out!)

And I came bloody close to losing my job too. Looking back now, I think my boss in the Civil Service knew what a bloody loser I'd turned into – rolling up still half-drunk every morning, doing a half-assed job until it was time to clock out and I could head back to the pub with my mates. He had more than enough ammunition to get rid of me three times over. I reckon he just couldn't be arsed with the paperwork.

A true civil servant.

Like all the best "loser" stories though, I did turn it around – but not before parting company with those five "mates" – guys who really didn't give a toss about me, or what I wanted out of life.

As long as I was there to buy the next round, and share in the taxi money, or divvy up a pizza, that was all they cared about.

They weren't friends. They were leeches. And they were literally sucking the life out of me. At the time we "went our separate ways" there was a massive barney (caused by my "best mate" sleeping with loads of people behind the back of one of my good friends – and me calling him out on it), and I was cast out – and I remember being utterly devastated at the time.

I thought I'd reached the low point of my life, and looking back now, I probably had. But whereas I could only foresee pain, heartache, and despair, shedding those "friends" was actually the best thing that could have happened to me, and the only way really was up.

I threw myself into work and started to sort my life out.

I tried (and failed) to win my fiancée back, but then, as I alluded to above, I met someone else. I wasn't even looking for anybody else at the time, but our eyes met across a crowded karaoke bar, and there was an instant attraction. That girl would go on to be the future Mrs Lamerton, the mother to my children, and the true love of my life. If I'd still been hanging around with those five losers though, she'd probably have been "a fun night" before she settled down with a real adult.

Best thing that ever happened.

I don't drink anymore, but I found myself in a pub a few months back, as Plymouth Argyle were on the telly in an away match in Newport on a Tuesday night the winner would play Liverpool at Anfield the following weekend.

(As I'm sure you remember, Plymouth Argyle won the game, and went on to produce one of the performances of the season, providing Liverpool with a defensive masterclass in a 0-0 draw at Anfield, before losing 1-0 in the replay at Home Park.)

And low and behold, who should I see in there, but my former "best mate", and a bunch of his cronies. They looked like crap – like they'd spent the best part of 20 years getting drunk every night.

Probably because they had. None of them was married. A few of them still lived with their parents. They were still in the same dead-end jobs they were in when I knew them. And they were still going out, living like true nineties lads – only it's 2017 now fellas – it's time to grow up.

There's no danger of those five muppets making it onto the Forbes rich list. Five more people that probably won't be on there (unless you're Sam Walton), are your friends and family. They're always the first to offer advice, and it really is meant with the best of intentions, but for most people, they really are the last people you should be listening to.

You can choose your experts, but you can't choose your family

If I'd listened to my friends and family back in 2001, you wouldn't be reading this book now. I wouldn't own any businesses. I would have no investments. I'd still be a civil servant.

I had a "nice secure job", a "job for life", with a "really good pension" – they couldn't understand why I wanted to give that up to pursue "this internet thing" that they didn't understand (why would they? They'd never run a business, let alone an online one!), and it would have been very easy for me to listen to them.

I was a naive, wet-behind-the-ears 22-year-old civil servant, and they had decades of experience of how the world worked – you study hard, you get a good job, you go for promotions, and you get a nice pension.

I must have been going through a rebellious streak, as I not only ignored their advice by quitting my job and starting my first business, but I also bought my first house, despite being told that "the housing market is overpriced. It's going to crash."

I bought my first house in 2000, paying £55,000, despite being told by family members that it was only worth "£35k, maybe £40k at most". We sold it three years later for £86,000. I made almost as much money just owning that house as I had done working the day job for those three years!

When it comes to property, my one regret is that I didn't ignore well-meant family advice earlier – I had the chance to buy a two-bed flat in around 1997. It was on the market for £13,500, and I had the deposit all saved, but I was talked out of it because "flats are hard to sell. You'll never get your money back".

Two years later my auntie bought that exact flat – for £25,000. If I still owned it today, my mortgage would be about £30 a month, and the flat would be worth around £100,000. But you can't take "would bes" to the bank.

I like you. I really do. I'm just not going to listen to a word you say

So many people take advice from their closest friends for one reason only – they like them. I've had to train myself now to know not only when to IGNORE people who I DO like, but also when I SHOULD listen to people I DON'T like.

You don't need to like someone to learn from them.

You can even strongly disagree with several of their viewpoints, and you don't have to follow their path exactly. I spent quite a lot of money going to a three-day event recently, with two massive rock-star headline speakers, whose main messages – the stuff they're peddling day in, day out, I REALLY strongly disagree with. I don't particularly like them as people. But do they have one or two nuggets of information that I can take out of it? You bet they do.

It's just like panning for gold. I'll happily sift through the shitty coloured water, and chuck back all the useless lumps of rock, just to get one or two small nuggets of pure gold.

 BIG IDEA...

You don't need to LIKE someone to learn from them.

Take Grant Cardone, the $500m real estate guy I mentioned earlier.

He's very intense. He works 100+ hour weeks and feels everyone else should too. You should work harder, hustle, grind, etc., etc. That goes completely against everything I stand for because we run what I call an "ambitious lifestyle business".

Everyone in our company works from home, but we are very ambitious – we just work around people's lifestyles. Most of the people in the company have got kids and we work around school runs, their kids being sick, sports days, assemblies, etc.

As far as Mr $500m is concerned, that's not a real business, and we've given up on our ambition; we have been treasonous to our potential.

It would be very easy to shut down, and just say "Well, he's wrong. He doesn't know anything about me or my life. There's nothing he can teach me."

But I just apply a filter – he's achieved my goals before, so clearly he's got something to teach me, so I need to know – am I willing to implement what he's teaching? And should I listen to everything he says or just one or two areas?

(Don't) read all about it

Someone I try not to listen to at all is the media. For me, it just breeds fear, hate, and negativity. I'll normally have a little chuckle whenever I see my in-laws, and they start a conversation with the immortal line "according to the Mail..." before telling me what's going to give me cancer, how we're all doomed, why the housing market is going to crash, what companies are going to go bust this year, how immigrants are taking all of our jobs, not to go to London because terrorists are there waiting to blow us all up, how there's a mugger on every street corner, and how all Big Issue sellers are fakes who drive Porsches and live in penthouse apartments.

This junk makes it into the papers because it sells papers.

"We're safer, healthier, wealthier and wiser than we've ever been" doesn't shift copies. Well, it might do for one day, but what do you write about the following day? The only way to sell newspapers is to sell negativity. Get Katie Hopkins to have a go at someone, preferably someone from a minority. Tell people that the stock market is going to crash, your house is going to lose value, and immigrants are coming over here, taking your jobs, and telling you how to live your life.

Every day's like Halloween when you read the papers. Scary stuff everywhere you look.

Don't buy negativity. I don't want negativity in my life, full stop. And I sure as hell don't want to pay 65p a day for the privilege.

Every Luke Skywalker needs a Yoda

I was very lucky when I first started my business – there were a number of people, who at first glance would appear to be my competitors – those who ran similar businesses to mine. And for some reason, they were happy to share tips, tactics, and ideas with me. They'd tell me where I was going wrong, and how I could improve my business and make more money.

(The reason they were happy to share so freely, was because they had a growth mindset, rather than a scarcity one. They knew that if everyone helped each other out, we'd all make fewer mistakes, and everyone's business benefitted – if someone helps me out, and my business grows as a result, theirs doesn't shrink – it actually grows too, as I then share something I've found with them – it's a virtuous circle!)

I didn't know it at the time, but these were my very first mentors – they're the people who gave me an arm around the shoulder when I needed it, and a kick up the arse when I needed that. They told me what worked, what didn't, and they probably saved me months and months of trying stuff that wouldn't work, and brought in many thousands of pounds of additional revenue in those crucial early years.

Knowing what I know about compounding now, I'm even more thankful for those first mentors (so thank you again Clarke and Jason – I certainly wouldn't be here without you. I'd probably be muddling along trying to scratch a living somehow!) – and if there's one piece of advice I can give anyone just starting out in their entrepreneurial career, it is to get a mentor as soon as you possibly can.

You don't necessarily need to start by paying for one in the early days – just get out there, talking to other successful business owners. Hang around in business forums and Facebook groups (like ours – www.bigidea.co.uk/facebook) and ask away.

The only "stupid question" is the one that you don't ask.

I've now got five or six mentors, who I pay a fair chunk of change to every year – why? Because they're specialists in areas where I generalise.

When I want to know about tax changes, I call my tax guy.

When I want to build complex marketing funnels, I get hold of my funnels expert.

I've got people I can call up and ask for their EXPERT advice on anything from nutrition and fitness, to Forex trading, social media, copywriting, networking, public speaking, and mindset.

If you wanted advice on any of those, who would you call?

WHY DON'T YOU...

"They load the clip in omnicolour
Said they pack the 9, they fire it at prime time
Sleeping gas, every home was like Alcatraz
And mutha f**kas lost their minds
No escape from the mass mind rape
Play it again jack and then rewind the tape
And then play it again and again and again
Until ya mind is locked in
Believin' all the lies that they're tellin' ya
Buyin' all the products that they're sellin' ya
They say jump and ya say how high
Ya brain-dead
Ya gotta f**kin' bullet in ya head."

Rage Against the Machine
Bullet in the Head

It was the Brit Awards last night

Do you know how I know that? No, I didn't watch it – I knew it was happening because my Facebook feed was full of people moaning about it. Yep, several of my "friends" (I use that term very loosely!) on Facebook were bemoaning the fact that:

1. The Brit Awards was on the telly and...

2. That they were watching it

In every single case, they took to their social media soapbox to let the whole world know that they were watching it, and they weren't enjoying a single minute of it. Whether it was "the state of music today", what the presenters were wearing, whether somebody was lip-syncing, how so-and-so has murdered a particular track, or just that they didn't know who any of these "celebrities" were, or why they were being given a prime time audience.

As far as I can tell, none of these people were being held at gunpoint and forced to watch the show.

Back when I was a kid (it wasn't that long ago, honest!), there used to be a TV show that I believe was only on during the school holidays, called "Why Don't You?". You may remember this program if you grew up in the '80s as I did – and you may recall the FULL title of the show (which wasn't referred to that often), which was "Why Don't You Turn Off Your Television Set, And Do Something Less Boring Instead?"

And for some reason, that was the line that came to me last night. Why on earth are these people, who are in complete control of their lives (unless I was mistaken, and they WERE being forced at gunpoint to watch Miley Cyrus pretend to sing whilst all her clothes fell off) CHOOSING to spend their precious free time watching something that they don't like?

They're sat there, staring at a 40-inch rectangle on the wall, and then picking up a 4.7-inch rectangle so they can tweet or post on Facebook about how much they're hating watching what's happening on the big rectangle. Then they keep on watching and keep on moaning, like a vicious circle of masochism, building to a frenzy that only a One Direction "performance" can provide.

You've got complete control over your life

How you choose to spend your time dictates the level of your success. What do you think is going to have a more positive impact on your life – watching Coronation Street, or watching a TED talk? Watching people attempt karaoke on X-Factor, or listening to podcasts?

 BIG IDEA...

Your brain is like a sausage-making machine.
If you put JUNK in, you'll get junk out.

Watching the Brit Awards (whilst moaning on social media about it), or reading a personal development book?

Are you spending more time with Tim Ferriss and Dan Kennedy, or Phillip Schofield and Ant and Dec?

Now don't get me wrong – I'm not completely anti-television, I do watch SOME TV. But I am anti-wasting-your-life. I limit myself to between 45 minutes and an hour of TV per day, and I'm watching high-quality, well-written US dramas like House of Cards, Mad Men, Breaking Bad, The Wire or The Sopranos.

I cancelled our Sky TV subscription last year, and it's up there as one of the best decisions I've ever made. By the time you added in multi-room, HD, Sky+, Sky Go etc., my monthly bill was getting close to £100 – and I wasn't even using it. The process of leaving Sky was an experience in itself – they make it really hard for you to leave without sitting through somebody on the retention team giving it the hard sell. In the end, I had to get shirty with them and tell them to just process the bloody cancellation – I want out!

They were like a drug dealer saying "go on, just have one more hit. I'll give you a month's supply for half price. I'll chuck in some extras" – they get people hooked, and then milk them for everything they've got. But the likes of Netflix, Now TV and Amazon Prime are disrupting this tired old model, and I'm predicting tough times ahead for Sky unless they adapt to these challengers.

I can pay Netflix £7.49 a month and watch high-quality programmes (many made exclusively by Netflix themselves) in HD, and in multiple rooms. The same service from Sky would set me back around £50 a month.

Those 45 minutes a day help me to relax and switch off from "business mode". By watching those high quality dramas (I once watched an episode of The Wire, directly followed by an episode of The Bill, which made the gap in quality from the US to our shores incredibly obvious), which have some of the best script writers in the world working on them, my copywriting naturally improves too – it helps me tell better stories myself.

By restricting myself to a diet of only high-quality, well-written US drama, I avoid the mind-numbing that can happen when you'll watch ANYTHING that's on. For some people, the TV is ALWAYS on – if they're awake, the telly's on. It's a constant companion for them.

They'll watch breakfast TV, the morning magazine shows, then the news at lunchtime. There might be a film on in the early afternoon, then it's time for the tea-time quizzes (three of them on three different channels), a quick bit of brainwashing with some more news, and then it's time to put your brain to sleep with the soaps – Emmerdale, then Corrie, then EastEnders. Then Corrie comes BACK on again, before Celebrity Paint Drying starts at 9pm, followed by some badly-written, badly-acted British "drama" that my seven-year-old could have written the "plot" for.

These people are feeding their minds with at least six or seven hours a DAY of inane, mind-numbing drivel. They're literally wasting their lives.

As I've said, I'm not totally anti-TV, but if you find yourself sat there staring at the big rectangle for hours on end, thinking to yourself "I'm not enjoying this", then why don't you...

Turn off your television set, and do something less boring instead?

TELLING FEAR TO F*** OFF...

"Fear kills more dreams than failure ever will."

Suzy Kassem

What are you afraid of? What keeps you awake at night? Public speaking? Picking up the phone? Closing a sale? Hiring staff? Firing staff? Doing the accounts? Dealing with technology? Running out of money? Clowns?

Whatever it is, I've got a tactic to help you conquer your fears. It involves a hula hoop, eating beans on toast, and jumping out of an aeroplane at 15,000 feet (thankfully not all at the same time!).

Careful now

As humans, we're only born with two built-in, pre-loaded fears – the fear of loud noises, and the fear of falling. Anyone who's had young children will attest to their fearless capabilities – most children feel able to do anything at all. They're off climbing trees without worrying about how high they are, running full pelt without really looking where they're going, happy to talk and laugh and sing, and strike up conversations with other children and adults who they've only just met.

But then before you know it, the conditioning starts. We dress it up as parenting. Pay close attention to the words used by parents of young children, and it won't be long before you hear these classics:

"Careful"

"Watch out"

"Don't do that"

"Don't talk to strangers"

"That's dangerous"

"You could hurt yourself"

"Slow down"

"Don't run"

"What would Mrs Teacher think if she saw you doing that?"

Then, of course, the little darlings get to school, and are ridiculed by their peers if they stand out, if they get a question wrong, or by the teacher if they do anything except "sit down, shut up and listen".

And then we wonder where these fears of speaking in public, of taking risks, of making mistakes, of what other people think, of every little thing, come from!

Learn to hula

One of my mentors used to say "The size of your comfort zone is equal to the size of your success. The bigger your comfort zone is, the more success you will have. The smaller you keep your comfort zone, the more you limit your success."

He used to demonstrate this really well, using a Hula Hoop (the big plastic ring, not the bag of crisps). He recognised that the key to growing your comfort zone lay in doing things that were JUST outside your comfort zone. He'd get me to imagine a fairly small hula hoop, that would only just fit around me, and got me to (metaphorically) lay it on the ground and stand in the middle of it.

"That represents your comfort zone," he would say. "You're completely at ease with doing everything inside of that hula hoop. But anything outside of the hoop scares you. The stuff just outside of the hoop scares you a little, and the stuff that's further away from you scares you more.

"The only way to grow your comfort zone is to do stuff that's JUST outside of the hula hoop – within your grasp, but certainly OUTSIDE of your comfort zone. Stuff that scares you, without a doubt, but don't even THINK about attempting the really scary stuff at this stage."

Once I'd done something that was JUST outside my hula hoop, he would give me a slightly bigger metaphorical hula hoop – "There you go. Your comfort zone just got bigger. Now if you want to grow it further, just keep doing stuff that's within your reach, but just outside of your hula hoop."

I remember thinking at the time "Yeah right, that seems a bit too easy", but figured what the hell, I had nothing to lose by just trying a few things.

I'd originally started working with him due to having quite low self-confidence around other people. Sure, I'd built up a successful business or two, but if anyone asked me what I did, I'd panic, go into a cold sweat, and mumble something about "Internet marketing". I knew that if I wanted to grow my businesses and investments to the next level, I needed to tackle this.

I knew that I needed to start JUST outside my comfort zone. It would do me no good whatsoever to go straight from being really timid and shy, being unable to speak with clarity and confidence to a single person to speaking on stage in front of 3,000 people for instance. So I looked at what scared me just a little bit. And I decided that was going to be talking to strangers.

I set myself the goal of starting a conversation with just ONE person, who I didn't previously know. That's a ridiculously simple goal. Anyone could talk to one person! And that's why it worked – I was aiming one centimetre outside my comfort zone, so I started with "let's just start ONE conversation with ONE person, ONE time." So easy, I literally couldn't fail.

 BIG IDEA...

Struggling to get started? Set a goal that's so damn easy you physically CAN'T fail – it'll give you the MOMENTUM to power on.

And I did it. And I loved it. I ended up chatting with that person for a good 20 minutes. We had some laughs, we told some stories, we talked about business and investing (my two favourite topics!), and it was easy. Bam! My hula hoop just got a little bigger...

So I pushed it. I set a goal to talk to one stranger per week. Then per day. Then at every opportunity. Then I took a public speaking course. Then I did a talk in front of 40 people. Then 100 people. Then I launched a podcast (www.bigidea.co.uk/podcast) and started talking to literally thousands of strangers, all over the world. I started doing live videos in our Facebook group (www.bigidea.co.uk/facebook).

Every time I did something JUST outside my comfort zone, my hula-hoop got bigger and bigger.

And low and behold, my mentor was right – as my comfort zone got bigger, so did the level of my success. Being willing to do stuff (whether that's public speaking, going to networking events, giving sales presentations, or doing live videos and podcasts) that you know is going to scare you, but you also know will move your business forward tremendously, will make a huge difference to your lifestyle.

 BIG IDEA...

Everything you desire lies JUST outside your comfort zone.

Keep growing your hula hoop

Just set a goal to do ONE thing, that's JUST outside your comfort zone. Think you can't do press-ups? Could you do ONE? Set a goal that's so easy, you can't fail. Can't do press-ups? Do one. But then keep stretching that goal, so one press-up becomes two. Two becomes five. Five becomes ten. Ten turns into twenty, and so on.

I now do things JUST to stretch that hula hoop. When I'm on a training course, I'll now sit in the front row rather than hide in the back; I'll be sure to ask questions, and maybe go and speak to the trainer during a break. I've started going to networking events, and actually talking to people rather than hiding in the corner, hoping for a friendly face.

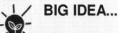
It's probably no exaggeration to say that I'm a hundred times more confident than I was just a few short years ago – I certainly wouldn't have had the balls to put my name to a book, and put it out there for people to shoot down before.

I recall a conversation with 'Er Indoors, about six months after I started growing my hula hoop – I'd arranged to drive across the country to go and watch a band from my youth playing a gig. I travelled on my own, stayed overnight, and we were discussing my plans for the day after the gig. "Oh, I might stop off and go skydiving on the way home," I said, rather casually.

"WHAT?"

"I said 'I might go skydiving on the way home' – there's this indoor skydiving place about 20 miles from the hotel I'm staying at. Either that, or I might go to the indoor ski-slope, and do some snowboarding."

"What's got into you recently?" she said. "You never used to do crazy stuff like this."

What had "gotten into me" was self-confidence. That was the moment I knew it was working. My hula hoop had grown so big that other people were starting to notice it.

The more you do stuff in your personal life to grow your comfort zone, the more success you'll have in business. And the more you do stuff to grow your business's hula-hoop, the more confident you'll feel in your personal life. The two feed off each other, like a virtuous circle. Just keep growing those hula-hoops.

Worry ye not

Have you ever kept yourself awake at night worrying about a presentation you've got to give the next day or an exam you're about to take?

What difference did worrying about it make, other than making you more stressed, with less focus, clarity, and energy due to the lack of sleep? If you're prepared, you're prepared. If you're not, you're not. Worrying about it now isn't going to change a damn thing.

You're either ready or you're not. You've either done everything you can to be ready for this, or you haven't. Whatever's going to happen is going to happen. Keeping yourself awake with worry only has negative consequences. The hard work was done months (and in some cases years) ago – the only thing you can do tonight to affect tomorrow's outcome is to ensure you turn up relaxed and rested. Go. To. Sleep.

Try playing ten to twenty minutes of Candy Crush, Tetris, or (my personal fave) Two Dots – something that engages your brain in a visual, problem-solving way – that stops your monkey brain going over the presentation or exam in your head over and over again, and literally FORCES it to focus on something else, something that REALLY doesn't matter, and which you can happily forget as you sail off into the land of nod.

I never actually did that indoor skydive in the end, but the idea was planted, so in the summer of 2016, I did the real thing instead – I jumped out of an aeroplane at 15,000 feet, just for the sole purpose of growing my hula-hoop.

Fear isn't logical

Thankfully, it wasn't until I'd completed the jump that I realised I'd completely put my life in the hands of a total stranger. I'd literally got on an aeroplane, and strapped myself to some bloke who I'd only met half an hour before. I didn't even ask him if he had a parachute on his back, if he'd checked that it was packed correctly, if he knew what he was doing, if he'd even DONE this before. I just trusted, that of course, he knows what he's doing.

I think that's because logically, I just knew that would be the case. They don't let the general public jump out of aeroplanes attached to someone who "fancies giving it a go", or who has messed up a few times when packing his chute. But fear isn't logical.

During the briefing in the morning, one of the instructors asked whether anyone was nervous. A few hands went up. (I kept mine down of course – stiff upper lip and all that. I was petrified.) "That's fine," says he. "It's perfectly normal to be a little nervous."

"By the way, did any of you arrive here in a car today?" Everyone's hand went up.

"Oh good, you've done the dangerous bit."

A brilliant way to use a bit of humour to settle the nerves. And of course, it's true. You are far more likely to die driving a car than you are doing a tandem skydive. Yet we don't let that stop us jumping in the steel coffin and driving it at 70mph every day, do we? That's because of the story you tell yourself:

> *"I've been driving every day for years, and never killed myself. But I read in the paper last week about a skydiver whose parachute didn't open, and he fell to his death."*

"According to the Mail..."

I now take the stance that if it's in the newspapers, I don't need to worry about it because the sheer fact that the newspapers are printing it means it's rare enough to be newsworthy.

The Daily Mail doesn't report, "191 people were killed by coronary heart disease yesterday." There WERE, on average 191 fatal heart attacks yesterday, but the papers didn't report on that. "Government on car crash high alert as fears that 2,000 people a year could die." Well, that IS how many people a year die in car crashes, but that doesn't sell newspapers, does it?

I may live in deepest darkest Devon, but every now and then I travel up to the big smoke (no, not Bristol!), and head to London for meetings, conferences, training courses and the like. I went there just before Christmas last year, which is a great time to visit, as all the Christmas lights are up, the "Winter Wonderland" bits and pieces are in place, and everyone seems to be that little bit happier and friendlier.

On this particular occasion, I was advised by a member of my family who shall remain nameless, (but she knows who she is!) not to go to London because, "according to the papers", Islamic extremist terrorists are planning to do something in London this Christmas. They're going to blow up tubes. They're going to plant bombs somewhere. They're going to drive a truck into a crowd or things.

"Something's going to happen in London and you're going to get caught up in it", she told me. Well, it's a good job these extremist terrorists had the foresight to send a press release out to the Daily Mail, informing the public of their plans, wasn't it?

I did a bit of research and said, "Actually, on any given day in London, there are about 10 million people there. The chances of me, one person, being caught up in an act of terrorism, me being the one in 10 million on one day, in one area of London is pretty tiny." In my case, I am infinitely more likely to be hit by a London bus than I am to be a victim of terrorism. But they don't warn you in The Mail or The Express, "There's a good chance that you might be hit by a London bus if you go to London" – probably because that wouldn't sell as many newspapers as spreading widespread panic and fear by making stuff up to scare the public does.

The chances of that "black swan" event like dying from doing a skydive, or being involved in a terrorist plot, actually happening are so small. If it's rare enough to be newsworthy it's either not going to happen, or it's not likely to happen to me. It's not actually likely to impact my life. My beliefs are that it's the stuff like heart disease or car crashes that they no longer bother to report – THAT'S the stuff that's more likely to get you.

Exiting the aircraft

Do you know what the scariest bit about that skydive was? It was the anticipation. It had built up during the day, as we had "typical British skydiving weather" – cloud, and lots of it. So whereas I was expecting to have no time to think about it – arrive at 8am, jump at 9am, back in the car by 10am, we were sat around with nothing to do but think about what was going to come (if the cloud ever buggered off).

Eventually, in the middle of the afternoon, the cloud broke, and the first planeload of people went up. After hours and hours of sitting around waiting, never sure whether we were actually going to be able to jump that day or not, suddenly it was "all systems go" – and before you know it, I'm suited up, I've had a quick chat with the bloke I'm going to be throwing myself out of the plane with, and I'm walking towards one of the smallest planes I've ever seen.

We climbed aboard and sat on this bench facing the "wrong way" – towards the tail end of the aircraft, which was covered in duct tape – never a reassuring sight, but hey at least I had a parachute! Before I knew it, we were in the air, beginning our ascent to 15,000 feet. No safety briefing, no trolley service. Just this see-through Perspex door that you know at some point you're going to have to exit the plane via – I've never boarded a plane before without the intention of still being on the plane when it lands!

We got above the clouds, and the instructor (who was behind me) tapped me on the shoulder. "Oh hell," I thought, "here we go" – but no, he was just letting me know that we were at 5,000 feet, and this was the point at which we'd open the parachute. We still had another 10,000 feet to climb, which would take about another five or six minutes. (It would only take us 60 seconds to cover that same distance on the way back down!).

I found myself sweating, breathing very shallowly, and generally bricking it pretty much from that point on. I didn't think I could be more scared.

I was wrong.

Suddenly, everyone around me started looking intently at their altimeters. Everyone started checking their equipment, and the instructor behind me started tightening up all the straps and equipment connecting us. The guy sat by the Perspex door opened it, and a blast of icy air and engine noise hit us.

Shit. Just. Got. Real.

The guy who had just opened the door peered out. The light above his head went green, and then he vanished. There was this "whoop" noise as he disappeared out of the door, never to be seen again – we were in a plane travelling at 90mph in one direction, and he was now falling at 120mph in the other direction.

Guess who was next?

If they'd offered me the chance, there and then, to pay an extra £100 and go back to my seat, and land with the plane, I honestly would have taken it. But I was almost at the point of no return. I was now being slid out of the plane by the instructor, a feeling of absolute terror completely taking over me. I could feel him rocking us as we prepared to go on the count of three.

1...

2...

The bastard went on two.

If you're a member of our Ambitious Lifestyle Business Facebook group (www.bigidea.co.uk/facebook), you'll see the above photo of my skydive on the welcome post – and if you delve deep, the video is there to watch too – and it's worth a viewing, just to see the look on my face develop, from one of pure terror to one of sheer, unadulterated joy, in about five seconds flat, as we exit the plane and begin our freefall.

It was quite possibly the best feeling I've ever had – the adrenaline flowing through your body, the shock of the noise, the feeling of flying, the amazing views. When we landed, I had a huge grin plastered all over my face – a grin that I saw replicated time and time again as my fellow jumpers landed.

And it all changed when I crossed that line from "I'm not sure I want to do this because it's scary" to "I'm doing it, and it's bloody brilliant". I'm forever telling my kids now that EVERYTHING is scary until you've done it once – then it's not scary anymore. Whether that's a big slide, a roller-coaster, asking a girl out, or jumping out of an aeroplane. You've just got to stop THINKING about it, and JUST BLOODY DO IT.

BIG IDEA...

The worst part of any fear is the ANTICIPATION. REDUCE the time between the idea and the action to combat this.

I was scared of THIS?

There's only one thing more ridiculous than being scared about something you want to do – and that's worrying about something that COULD happen. Again it's the years of conditioning from parents, friends, and family, and the media warning you about the horrors that could befall you.

If this is something that affects you, why not try out exactly what it is you're afraid of, in a controlled environment, for a limited time?

Worried that you're going to go broke and lose all your money?

Go rent a tiny bedsit for a week and eat nothing but Tesco Value beans on Tesco Value toast, allowing yourself £1 a day to live on. Seven days later, you'll realise that it wasn't half as bad as your mind had made it out to be, and "going broke" is no longer scary, as you now know you would survive, and be able to start again.

Maybe you're concerned about what other people think of you?

Spend a week wearing the most ridiculous clothes that you can find in the charity shop. For the first few days, you'll be enormously self-conscious, you'll notice every stare and sideways glance, and your friends and family will tease you mercilessly. But by the end of the week, you just won't care. Your friends will have grown tired of ribbing you, and you'll realise the most important thing – you are still you, and you don't need the approval of others to be the best version of yourself.

 BIG IDEA...

Once you've DONE what you're afraid of, you'll wonder why you were ever afraid of it.

Another tactic I've used to expand my hula-hoop is "going first" – if I'm at an event, and they ask for a volunteer, my hand shoots right up. "Anybody got any questions?" Yep, right here. Again, this eliminates the time spent anticipating how scary it's going to be, and just getting on with doing it, before you get the chance to be scared! It's much more relaxing to just be the first volunteer and have some fun, rather than spending the next few minutes avoiding eye contact and thinking "I hope he doesn't pick me".

Want to speak to a pretty girl? Go first.

Want to make a good connection at a networking event? Go first.

Want to be closer to your family? Go first.

Want a better relationship with your partner? Go first.

Wish people smiled on the tube? Go first (that one might get you some strange looks!).

Go. First.

Expand that hula-hoop.

F*** Fear.

FAT, SICK, AND STRESSED TO THE EYEBALLS?

"You'd better look after your mind, and you'd damn well better look after your body. They need to last you a lifetime."

Warren Buffett

This picture of health was me in 2003, aged 26, but looking 46 – about five stone overweight, with a fag hanging out of my mouth, and a glazed-over look from too much booze. Quite how I was fighting all the ladies off at this point, I'll never know.

Never mind health warnings on cigarettes – they should plaster that picture on crates of beer

If you were to look up the words "heart attack waiting to happen" in the dictionary (assuming the dictionary has started listing entire phrases now rather than the more traditional words), you may well have seen this picture staring back at you. Dead man walking.

You see, life was good in 2003. I'd started making some serious money in the business, was jetting off around the world to conferences and meetings, and had just moved into our dream house. I was the golden boy, who had the Midas touch – everything I touched turned to gold.

But I was so focused on the business, that I completely ignored my health. My diet consisted of takeaways, frozen ready-meals, beer, and kebabs. My idea of exercise was walking to the post box once a day (well, I was smoking 20 cigarettes a day, so at least it got me out of breath!) – sure I wasn't sleeping that well at night, but I put that down to not being able to shut off the entrepreneurial idea-generating part of my brain, and found that I could self-medicate myself off to the land of nod by administering five or six cans of lager every night.

I was literally eating, over-working, smoking and drinking myself into an early grave. But hey, at least I would be able to afford a REALLY nice grave, and I now had the perfect "before" photo.

Sarah and I were trying to start a family around this time, and it just wasn't happening (can't imagine why... I was in amazing shape, really looking after myself, so my virility must have been through the roof!) – so I started to worry about that too.

And then "Mr Midas Touch" turned into "Mr Bean" – everything I touched business-wise went to shit. The harder I worked, the less effective I was. The business went from making £25k a month profit to losing £10k a month in the space of six months, and there was a very real possibility that I might lose the business, and with it, my dream house.

So now I had something to REALLY worry about. So of course, I worked harder. And "self-medicated" harder. And got sick.

I developed flu-like symptoms and a blotchy rash all over my body. I went to the docs – "Are you under any stress at all?" they asked. Hmm, let me think – just a little! Turns out I was having an "acute, short phase of a disorder with features of depression or anxiety" – or what you and I might call a nervous breakdown.

So there I was – fat, sick, and stressed to the eyeballs, making myself feel "better" with alcohol, caffeine, and nicotine. Something had to change, or I'd be joining my sister in the graveyard soon.

I am a quitter

First to go were the smokes. I'd like to say there was some altruistic reason for quitting, but in the end, it came down to me being tight with money. I'd been buying packs abroad for £1.50 a pack, and refused to pay UK prices (which at the time were around £5.50 a pack) when I ran out of the cheap ones. Thanks to "Mr Bean" running things in the business, foreign travel wasn't on the agenda anytime soon, and the ciggies were one expense I could certainly do without.

I'd given up (for all of nine months before taking a job with the CSA, which got me started again) a few years before using nicotine patches, so decided to give them a whirl again – and it was a nightmare (maybe because I was quite a bit more stressed than last time!), so I ended up using the patches AND a nicotine inhaler – and even then I found it really, really difficult for those first few days.

I think what kept me going was knowing that I simply couldn't afford to pay for a £5.50 a day habit (good job I never got onto hard drugs innit!) and that I'd done it before, so I knew it was possible. I downloaded a Quit Smoking Calculator, which kept track of how long it was since I'd stopped, how much money I'd saved (my big motivator!), and how much longer I was going to live (a happy by-product!). Interestingly, I've just run it now, and I've not smoked 75,920 cancer sticks, saving me more than £21,000 (at the 2006 prices – I was in a petrol station the other day and wanted to see how much a pack of 20 costs now – it was £9.50, so I've actually saved more like £35,000 to £40,000 over the last eleven years by giving up), and crucially, I've added as many as ten years to my expected lifetime. Ten years! By giving up before I hit 30, I should be able to avoid premature death as a result of my old habit completely.

So... smoking was gone – time to get in shape now, even more so after giving up the smokes. Suddenly you can actually TASTE food again, and you need to do something with your hands, so, like a lot of recent ex-smokers, I took up the habit of shovelling food into my gob 20 times a day instead.

I cut back on the frozen, processed meals, and started eating some real food. I stuck an exercise bike in my office. I set a vague goal like so many before me to "lose some weight" – and lose "some" I did – but still not enough. I was still finding it really tough – I was working very hard at being healthy, but then undoing it all at the weekends, working through a crate of beer and/or a couple of bottles of wine, plus the associated junk food that you eat when you're drunk.

Just those few changes though (giving up smoking, eating a little bit better and getting a little exercise) made quite a big difference to my health – enough that on the 22nd August 2009, Sarah gave birth to Jack Robert Lamerton, the child that we had been trying for – for the previous six years.

My best ever drunken purchase

Jack was due to be born in the middle of August, but we had been warned that he could be as much as four weeks early or two weeks late. Therefore, during this time I had to be on "hospital-run duty", which meant that I was completely teetotal from the start of July until the 22nd August (yes, we went out to "wet the baby's head" on the day he was born!) – around six weeks with zero booze – unheard of for me, and the longest I'd gone without any since I was 15.

The funny thing was when I started drinking again after my maternity-enforced ban, I found that my taste buds had changed – and I now found all lager repulsive! I recall sitting in a bar working my way through their drinks menu trying to find something that I didn't find disgusting – eventually, I found there were only two drinks that I didn't hate – Guinness, and red wine (not in the same glass!).

A few years later, I did a month-long "dryathlon" (where you don't drink for a month, to raise money for charity) – and again, when I tried to start drinking again, I found it really hard to enjoy the taste of anything alcoholic. But I persevered, persuading myself that what I needed was more expensive bottles of wine. After all, the more it costs, the better it would taste, right?

Things then came to a head on a Saturday night at the start of November. It was the weekend, so of course, I opened a bottle of wine. Sarah wasn't keen on red wine, so I had this bottle to myself. The first glass tasted awful. The second not much better. "Just as well finish the bottle," I thought as I poured the third.

With that bottle gone, literally leaving a bad taste in my mouth, I made what seemed at the time to be a perfectly logical decision – to open a second bottle of wine. After all, I need to wash the horrible taste of this first bottle away, and this different brand couldn't be as bad as the first one, could it? It could. Didn't stop me finishing the bottle though.

And there I sat, in my home office, at 3am on a Saturday night, on my own, pissed as a fart on god-awful wine. I felt truly disgusted with myself – I had just drunk TWO bottles of horrible wine, for no reason other than "It is Saturday". What a loser.

And then I made what I now describe as "my best ever drunken purchase" – I went on Amazon and searched for books on cutting down on drinking. I found one called "Kick the Drink... Easily" by Jason Vale, and decided to read it the next day once I'd got over the hangover and sobered up a touch – little did I know that this book was to change my life and that I was to get to know Jason Vale's work very well over the coming year.

I started reading the following day, with the sole intention of "drinking a bit less" – maybe every other weekend, or just once a month. But then I found myself nodding along enthusiastically like a bloody Churchill dog as Jason made an emotional, and logical case for not drinking at all. Everything was written in plain English, and in such a way that your brain gets rewired.

I honestly never thought that a book could cause me to never WANT to drink again – but that's exactly what happened. Jason even tells you that you SHOULD carry on drinking whilst reading the book, but I think after reading the first four or five chapters, my mind was made up – "I'm never going to drink again" – it just doesn't make sense to drink what is now programmed in my brain as "fruit-flavoured poison".

Jason introduces himself as "the juice master", which is a bit cringeworthy but does give you the idea that instead of killing your body's cells with poisonous alcohol, you could flood it with nutrients. Nice idea mate, but I think I'll start by swapping the red wine and Guinness for a nice cold Cherry Coke on a Saturday night for now.

Drink your greens

Through a combination of regular gym work and cutting out most processed and junk foods, I managed to lose a couple of stone from my bulk, and almost looked like I was made of something other than blubber. I thought I was doing ok, until the doctor called me in for a "regular check-up" (how can it be "regular" if you've never had one before?) – anyway, she checked my height, weight, blood pressure, all "not bad" – then took some blood for analysis and away I went.

Two weeks later, I get a phone call from the doctor – "I need to speak to you about your blood results. Your cholesterol is a bit too high. I'll send you a leaflet on how to lower it."

The leaflet never arrived, so I ended up playing doctor myself and asked the internet how to lower cholesterol:

Red wine is good for lowering cholesterol. Hmm, maybe I've caused a spike in my levels by giving up the sauce?

Getting more exercise helps. I already go to the gym three times a week – don't think I can do much more.

The biggest thing you can do – eat more fruit and veg.

Urgh.

I'll have the odd apple, a couple of bananas a week. That's my fruit intake.

Veg-wise? Carrots and peas with Sunday roast. And...

Erm... yeah, that's about it.

I don't really like any other veg.

How the hell can I get more fruit and veg in me, when I don't really LIKE eating fruit and veg?

If only there was a magic pill or a drink I could take that would give me all the nutrients I need, without having to munch on celery, or consume cabbage.

Wait a minute – there is a drink. The "Juice Master" does just that – he juices fruit and veg, and "floods his body with nutrients" – that's EXACTLY what I need to do.

So I head to Amazon, buy another Jason Vale book (this time on juicing), and a cheap juicer. I decide to start just after Christmas, so read the book whilst munching on Mint Matchmakers and leftover Christmas cake. It seems to have the same "brain-washing" power over me as the "kick the drink" one – and before you know it, I've added wheat flour, refined sugar, added salt, caffeine, and milk to the list of things I'm "never going to eat again", and have bought more fresh fruit and veg in one trolley-load than I did in the previous year.

The results were almost instant – the best sleep I've ever had, more energy, better skin, hair, nails, brighter eyes. I found myself more alert, more focused. And the weight just kept dropping off me as I replaced my go-to lunch (beans on toast or egg on toast) with a "turbo with a kick" (a juice consisting of apple, pineapple, ginger, celery, broccoli stem, cucumber, avocado, spinach). I go on to lose another two stone, have my cholesterol re-checked in the summer (better than it's ever been), and end the year by running the Plymouth 10k – on the exact day that I'd given up the booze 12 months earlier.

Reboot mind and body – at 110°c

Around the same time, I discovered the powerful impact that regular saunas had on me – I originally went a few times after a HIIT session at the gym, to relax those tired muscles. I found that I was coming out of the intense heat feeling really refreshed and relaxed, so it became a bit of a habit.

I then noticed that I went an entire year without getting so much as a cold. This is why the Finnish people love saunas – it flushes out all those toxins that your immune system would otherwise need to fight (a runny nose, cough, and fever sweats are your body's way of getting it out – a sauna replicates that fever sweat, so the slightest hint of anything bad is flushed out before it's had a chance to take hold.)

I also found that I was more alert the rest of the time. My focus and particularly my problem-solving had also improved immensely. I pretty much developed the ability to walk into the sauna with a huge problem that I couldn't figure out, and walk out 20 minutes later with the answer.

I believe the mind is like a computer browser – during the working day, we open up all these new tabs as we start working on different things, and have different conversations. Every time we check email, another couple of tabs open up. We spend some time on Facebook, and five more open up. We start thinking about all the potential things we COULD do within the business, and before we know it, we've got 75 open tabs in the browser.

Have you ever tried to use a computer that has 75 open tabs? It's slow, inefficient, and bloody infuriating at times. And so it is with your mind. For me, stepping into the sauna closes all those open tabs, and allows me to then open up just ONE new tab, and focus 100% of my mental energy on it.

It's almost like rebooting your computer – powering off all those open tabs in your head, and doing nothing except thinking. I use saunas for this exact purpose, as you're physically unable to do ANYTHING except sit, and quietly think in that heat – All your other senses are turned off (or right down) – it's dead quiet, there's hardly any light, and you relax intently – almost in a meditative state.

This is how most of the BIG technological and scientific breakthroughs came about. Newton didn't discover gravity whilst pulling an all-nighter – he was napping under a tree. Archimedes' famous "Eureka!" moment wasn't thanks to the power of his "hustle" – he was sat in the bath. Elon Musk came up with the idea for Tesla whilst sat on the toilet. OK, I might have made that last one up!

Abraham Lincoln famously said, "Give me six hours to chop down a tree, and I'll spend the first four sharpening the axe."

I was at an event recently where Gary Vaynerchuk was headlining. If you've ever watched any of Gary Vee's videos, you'll know that his attitude to business is somewhat different to mine (nay, the polar opposite I would say!) – he's a big fan of the "hustle", and this event was no different, with him regaling the audience with tales of how he worked every single Saturday for 12 years straight, as though it were a badge of honour, and advising someone who was struggling to find the time for all this hustling to "just sleep less".

Now Gary Vee knows a thing or two (you don't end up running a $100m per year business otherwise), but for me, he's an outlier – the exception rather than the rule. For most people, just working harder and harder (at the expense of your health) is hands down some of the dumbest advice I've ever seen given out.

Taking time out of your daily grind to do some quality thinking will sharpen your axe – whether that's shutting yourself away in a sauna, walking the dog, or even just popping a "Do not disturb" sign on the door for 10 minutes. Go sharpen your axe. Have your own "Eureka!" moment. Just watch out for falling apples.

Lammo's healthy life hacks

It's now four years since I picked up that "kick the drink" book that kick-started all of this, and I'm still alcohol-free, nicotine-free, and caffeine-free. I'm also mostly sugar-free, dairy-free and wheat-free, but do allow myself the odd "cheat day".

I now have a set of life-hacks that enable me to (fairly) easily keep healthy, without having to live on salad, and spend every spare minute in the gym. It also means that I can blow out on burgers and milkshakes every now and then!

BIG IDEA...

Being HEALTHY doesn't need to be hard. Find the hacks that work for YOU.

1. DRINK YOUR VEG. I still have either a freshly extracted fruit and veg juice or blend up a smoothie with loads of greens every day. Flood your body with nutrients.

2. DON'T POISON YOURSELF. Restrict the things that your body DOESN'T need (and expends energy removing from the body) – alcohol, nicotine, caffeine, dairy, wheat, anything "refined" or processed.

3. GET EIGHT HOURS SLEEP EVERY NIGHT. Don't burn the candle at both ends. Remember it's about working effectively. Sleep is when your body repairs itself and your mind processes things.

4. STAY HYDRATED. Oil stops the engine from seizing up. Water stops your brain from doing the same, and increases your metabolism, and flushes out toxins. I aim for three litres a day – one in the morning, one in the afternoon, and one in the evening.

5. STAY ACTIVE – EVERY DAY. For me, this is walking an average of 10,000 steps every day (having a dog helps a LOT with this – they'll want to go "walkies" even when you don't!), swimming twice a week, and hitting the gym at least once a week for a HIIT session.

6. REBOOT. I take a sauna for my "reboot" every day. But you don't need access to 110°c heat – this could be walking the dog, reading some fiction, meditation, or just sitting quietly and doing nothing for 15 minutes. Reboot those open tabs!

7. DON'T WORRY. Easier said than done, but if you can do something about it, then you don't need to worry. And if you can't do anything about it, then what's the point in worrying?

8. DON'T FORGET TO LAUGH. Laughter really is the best medicine. I love to have fun, and I really believe that life is to be enjoyed, not endured!

We started this chapter with the horrible "before" photo from 2003, so it makes sense that we end it with the "after" photo, which is below – this was taken in 2017, so 14 years later.

Yet I would argue that I look younger in the more recent photo – I certainly actually have some cheekbones that were buried under layer and layer of face-flab in the first photo. And I no longer have more chins than a Chinese telephone directory!

> *"If you don't look after your health, you'll have nowhere to live."*
>
> *Jason Vale*

MAGIC INGREDIENT #5 – ACTION!
(A.K.A. GETTING THE RIGHT SHIT DONE...)

"What you KNOW doesn't mean shit. What do you DO consistently?"

Tony Robbins

Which of the following do you think would make more money?

1. A beautifully scripted piece of direct mail followed up with a 9-step email follow-up campaign, interspersed with text messages, social media posts and telesales calls (where the initial direct mail piece never gets sent as it's "not quite perfect")

or

2. A badly-written email, knocked out in 20 minutes, complete with spelling mistakes, leading to a landing page which is poorly designed, and zero follow up (but the email actually gets sent?)

Imperfect ACTION trumps perfect inaction every time.

 BIG IDEA...

Imperfect ACTION trumps perfect INACTION every time.

Sure, there's great margins to be made in improving the conversion rate of every element of your sales funnel, but at some point, you have to actually send the bloody sales letter out, pick up the damn phone, put that Facebook ad live and open the door to your store.

There's only so much "tweaking" you can do before you've just got to say f*** it, and hit send.

Ask for what you want, and do what you say you're going to do

Do you want a promotion? To win a new customer? Get an old one to come back and buy again? Want to get a girlfriend (or boyfriend)?

If you don't ask, you don't get. You've already got the "no", and the only way you're gonna change that "no" to a "yes" is by taking ACTION, and asking for what you want. If you don't take ACTION, you don't get.

I think I've done well to get this far into the book without getting political, but it would be remiss of me to be writing about action without mentioning one of the greatest action-takers of the modern day political arena, Donald Trump – or to give him his proper title, PRESIDENT Trump. If ever there's a more perfect example of the "American Dream" that literally ANYONE can become President than "The Donald", then I've yet to see it.

He certainly isn't afraid to ask for what he wants – and nine times out of ten he gets it. If you've studied any of his business dealings from his life before he decided that he was somehow suitably qualified to run the country, you'll know that he does much more than "ask for what he wants" – he asks for MORE than he wants – and then negotiates back down to what he ACTUALLY wanted in the first place. I can only presume that he asked to be President because he really wanted to be a Senator, but amazingly, the people of America took him seriously. I know he's a confident man, but did he really expect to win?

Like him or loathe him (and there's a whole lesson there about not standing on the fence, trying to be everything to everyone), you can't accuse him of not taking action. Since he took office (around six months ago as I write this), barely a day goes by without him issuing a brand new Executive Order, bringing some new law in, or at least trying to. Most politicians have two goals in life:

1. Get elected
2. Get re-elected

Trump's plan seems to be:

1. Get elected by promising to take huge action
2. Do what you said you were going to do

Whether that's enough to get him re-elected in 2020, who knows.

But if you're running a small business, that second point is something you can deploy to your advantage and use to completely obliterate your competitors.

Just DO what you say you're going to do.

It sounds so basic, but most business owners don't do the simple things like calling customers back when they said they would, following up on leads, or giving a crap about the customer once the sale's been made.

Just take my damn money already!

I hired a gardener last year. When I was looking for one, I contacted seven different companies via their websites – I sent emails and left messages with their staff. How many of those seven even bothered to get back to a potential new customer?

None.

Not a single one.

If you want a million pound business idea, here's one – set up a gardening business in South Devon, and respond to customer enquiries, because none of your competitors will. You'll have the entire marketplace to yourself, and therefore can charge whatever you want!

Back in 2015, I had a small piece of cosmetic surgery (no, it wasn't a boob job!), and when researching potential clinics I found a plethora of them advertising on Google. They all had fancy websites, lead-capture forms, and plenty of information for those considering surgery. I wanted to compare the clinics against each other, so I completed online lead-generation forms with five different clinics.

I never heard from two of those clinics ever again. I estimate that they were paying somewhere in the region of £3.50 per click for the terms I'd searched for – and then they were just ignoring the leads.

Talk about money down the drain!

Another two DID get back to me – one of them sent me a single email with a brochure in it, and then never contacted me again. And the other one invited me to attend a consultation at their offices in Exeter, where I spent about an hour talking to a consultant about what I wanted, how it all worked, the next steps etc.

In other words, he had everything he needed to close the sale. All he needed to do now was to give me the price and ask for the sale. Job done.

A week later he emails me the price and says he'll call to find out what I want to do.

Guess what?

He didn't call.

I called him... twice! I left him voicemails along the lines of "Would you like to take my money?" – and I never heard from him again.

All four companies were PAYING money to get my business. And then they were all taking absolutely no action once I was there. They're probably grumbling now about how "advertising doesn't work" or about how expensive Google Adwords is these days, when the fact remains that if they actually did something as simple as "doing what they said they were going to do", they'd massively increase their conversion rate, and those Google ads would appear cheap by comparison.

 BIG IDEA...

Beat your competitors, just by DOING what you SAID you would.

In the end, therefore, I chose the clinic for my procedure based almost entirely on one factor – after paying for my attention, they went to the trouble of asking for the sale. But even they very nearly managed to well and truly balls that up – I had a telephone conversation with one of their consultants, and made it very clear where I was on the buying journey – I was pretty much ready to go with my credit card in my hand. I was giving off buying signals left, right and centre.

"Shall I call you again in a few weeks, once you've had a chance to think it over some more?" asks the so-called salesman. Erm, hell no!

Given my experience of the previous four companies, I've got a suspicion that if I hang up this phone now without having given you my card details, that I'm never going to see or hear from you ever again. Just take my damn money already!

Rather stunned that someone who searched Google for exactly what he was selling, would actually be interested in buying what he was selling, the sales guy somehow stumbled through the rest of the call, taking my payment details and booking me into the clinic for six weeks later. He explained that the surgeon would do one procedure now and that if I needed further surgery (which was likely), that could be repeated twice more, at a minimum of 12-month intervals.

I had the surgery, and as expected, the surgeon informed me that I would require a second procedure 12 months later, once this one had healed. "Darren (the sales consultant) will arrange that during your post-op follow-up", he said.

Do you think I ever heard from Darren again?

Well, it's been two years so far, and I'm still waiting.

The surgery cost £5,000. I could potentially have another two procedures, so that's £10k that Darren's just left on the table when all it would take for him to land that £10k sale is to take one simple piece of ACTION – to do what he said he would do, and follow up with me.

Why didn't Darren phone me after seven or eight months, ask me how I'm healing up, and ask whether I'd like to book that next op in the diary?

I was paying for the initial op on a 12-month interest-free finance, so he didn't even need to ask me to find a £5k lump sum – just a simple "Would you like to continue your monthly payments for another year, and I'll get you in the diary now?" would have done. One simple action – maybe a four-minute phone call, for a £5k sale.

Instead, he's probably off chasing new business and still making a right pig's ear of it, along with everyone else in that sector. He's taking action, he's keeping busy, but he's not taking the RIGHT actions – the things that will actually get money in the bank!

I'm forever correcting people in our Facebook group when they talk about "getting shit done" – and I remind them that it's not about "getting any old shit done", it's about getting the RIGHT shit done.

The first four magic ingredients (goals, desire, knowledge and environment) will help you figure out exactly what the right shit is for you.

Once you know that (and ONLY then!), then it's finally time to...

JFDI.

Just F***ing Do It.

Too many people repeat this mantra, without knowing what the "It" is that they're supposed to be doing. The saying isn't "Just F***ing Do Something" or "Just F***ing Do Anything", and the aim isn't to be busy. You should be aiming for effectiveness, rather than efficiency – to achieve one or two really meaningful things that move the needle forward rather than "inbox zero" or a nice completed "to-do" list.

Take the right actions, methodically, habitually, and you will propel your business in the right direction – to the lifestyle you've designed for yourself.

Take any old action, and who knows where you might end up.

Take no action, and you'll either stay exactly where you are or more likely, you'll go backwards – there is no status quo. You're either growing, or you're shrinking.

How do you ensure that you regularly take the right action?

Here's the process I use:

1. Create my "could do" list. This is a brain-dump of literally every idea I've had, every shiny new object, marketing idea, potential JV, and campaign that I COULD do. As ideas come to me throughout the year, I never immediately start work on them – they

always get added to the "could do" list first. Writing down everything that I COULD do ensures that no idea gets forgotten, and it also frees up brain space for me to focus on my key tasks.

2. Every 90 days, I take my "could do" list, and plan out my 90-day goals for the upcoming quarter (see chapter 4 – magic ingredient #1 – goals for more information on this process), creating my "big three" goals for the quarter.

3. I then break down those "big three" into monthly stepping stones – three per month (so nine in total), these are the "baby steps" that will move me towards the big three on a monthly basis.

4. Those monthly stepping stones then get further distilled into my weekly ONE THING. As the name suggests, that's just ONE task that if I achieve nothing else in the working week, I'm still on track to achieve the monthly stepping stone, which means I'm on track to achieve the big three, which means I'm on track to deliver the lifestyle I'm designing for myself.

5. I then work with an accountability partner to hold me accountable for that ONE THING. Just the sheer act of telling another human being "I'm going to do x, y, or z" is scientifically proven to result in an improved likelihood of hitting your goal. That's why having a "gym buddy" works. That's why having a "study partner" is encouraged. That's why group accountability such as Weight Watchers and Alcoholics Anonymous has such great success.

6. I focus on the actions, not the results. If you want to lose 20 lbs of body fat, and set a goal of doing cardio for 20 minutes, three times a week, sleeping eight hours every night, swimming 1km twice a week, and eating clean six days a week, then it's THOSE ACTIONS that you should focus on and track. You KNOW that if you follow that plan to the letter, you will lose weight and get healthier. But most people track the results (the numbers on the scales).

There's often a lag between taking the action and getting the results, which most people don't consider. So in the above example, you may have a week where you only do cardio twice a week, average seven hours sleep a night, don't make it to swimming, and only eat clean on four days. But then you stand on the scales and you've lost two pounds

– result! You appear to have got the desired results without taking the required action, but you've forgotten about the lag, and if you carry on not doing the actions that you know are required, the results are going to dry up.

Even worse than that is the week where you hit all your action targets – you've literally followed the plan to the letter. If you were scoring your actions out of 100, you'd score 110. But then you stand on the scales and see a half-pound gain.

WTF!

You've forgotten the lag again, only this time that lag has totally demoralised and demotivated you. You think to yourself "Why the hell am I starving myself and sweating my arse off, only to put weight on?" – so you revert to eating burgers and milkshakes again, only for the lag effect from that "110 out of 100" week to kick in, and you've lost weight that week – only now, you (wrongly) attribute that to the burger and milkshake diet, coupled with the "sit on the sofa watching TV" exercise regime, and give up your plan altogether.

Don't focus on the results. Focus on the ACTION. Design a plan that you KNOW will give you the results, and focus on (and track) the actions that you need to take to accomplish the plan.

The results will look after themselves, and there's only one way you can influence the results – by taking the ACTION regularly and habitually – week in, week out.

Want me to turn you into a kick-ass ACTION taker?

For a while now, I've been working with a number of small business owners, helping them design their business around their lifestyle, and helping them to get more of the RIGHT shit done.

99% of small business owners are running around like headless chickens, constantly chasing shiny new objects, working harder and harder, and like hamsters on wheels, they're getting nowhere fast. They're certainly not living the lifestyle they imagined when they first went into business. If you're anything like me, you probably thought it would be all private jets and private islands by now.

If that sounds like you, then I've got three bits of advice for you:

1. It's YOUR fault
2. You CAN change
3. We can HELP

That's why I created the One Percent Club.

99% of small business owners think the answer to their prayers is working harder. The One Percent know it's about working smarter. The 99% rock up at their desk every morning, and THEN decide what to do with their day. One Percenters plan in advance and control their day.

The 99% aren't living the lifestyle they want.

Why not join the one percent? If you join the One Percent Club, you'll get:

- My "World Domination" planner – this contains the ACTUAL tools that I've used to increase my business eight-fold in the last few years. You'll get the "could do" list, 90-day goal planners, the big three, stepping stones, and weekly "ONE THING" planners.
- Your very own accountability partner – someone to hold your feet to the fire, and to make sure you DO what you say you're going to do.
- Monday Meetups – a weekly online coaching call, where you can ask me anything you need to know about growing your business, designing your lifestyle, or critiquing your marketing.
- Access to a private Facebook group, where you can get direct access to myself and the whole of the Big Idea team, as well as your fellow One Percenters.
- Exclusive videos and training from me. You'll learn everything I learn.

Because I like to really get to know our One Percenters' businesses inside-out, I only take on TWELVE new One Percenters every 90 days.

If you go to www.bigidea.co.uk/opcc-book, you'll see a video from me, and one of two things:

1. If applications for the One Percent Club are currently open, you'll see a link to join.

or

2. If we're not currently accepting applications, then you'll see a link to join the waiting list. People on the waiting list will get priority when we do open the doors again.

Are YOU ready to join the one percent?

I THINK I'VE JUST HIIT MYSELF...

"I'm not really good at knowing where 85 or 90 percent is. I only know where zero and one hundred is."

Dorian Yates
Six-time Mr Olympia

I'll be the first to admit that my knowledge of bodybuilders, and in particular Mr Olympia winners is somewhat small – ask me to name three of them, and I'd probably have given you Arnie's name three times. But I've recently listened to a couple of podcasts where Dorian Yates, (whose quote I've used above) has been interviewed.

A brief history of HIIT

Now whilst I do have a passing interest in educating myself about health and fitness, I'm not a gym-freak, and I don't tend to listen to bodybuilding or any weight-training podcasts. No, I was listening to two separate BUSINESS podcasts, when Mr Yates popped up within a few weeks of each other.

So what made Dorian of interest to two separate high-profile business podcasters?

Well for one, Dorian Yates achieved things that he shouldn't have. He wasn't a natural bodybuilder. He didn't have the right physique for it. He didn't hang around with the right people, and he didn't come from the right background. And whilst he was following in the footsteps of Mr Schwarzenegger, he certainly wasn't following Arnie's training plan.

Whereas the Terminator would spend an average of four or five hours per day lifting in the gym (Arnie's mantra for success was pretty much "reps, reps, reps") Dorian found that he could achieve the best results for his goals within an hour. He'd work at a really high intensity –

putting the maximum amount of strain possible on each muscle group he wanted to target, for a really short period of time.

And then he'd rest.

His muscles would break down from the stress of being worked to a very high intensity, well beyond their normal capabilities, and then repair themselves over the rest days. But they wouldn't just repair the muscle groups to the state they were before – his body would recognise the intensity that they were previously worked at, and grow new fibres and tissue to allow for this increased stress without breaking down next time – hey presto: bigger muscles!

There wasn't a term for it at the time, but what Dorian Yates was doing back in the 90s was what we now know as HIIT – high-intensity interval training.

If you've caught any of Joe Wicks (The Body Coach) online or on TV recently (and if you haven't, where have you been for the last 12 months... he's been literally everywhere!!), you'll know that Joe Wicks likes four things:

1. Sharing photos of himself somewhere exotic with his shirt off

2. Calling broccoli "midget trees" (I love Joe for this alone, as it's got my kids eating broccoli!)

3. Making 15-second videos of healthy, tasty food that's cooked in one pan, and shouting "and that right there is lean in 15!" at the top of his voice

4. High-intensity interval training

As with Dorian Yates, Joe is turning the nonsense that traditional personal trainers have been saying for years on its head – getting and staying fit and healthy isn't about eating nothing but salad, and running on a treadmill for an hour.

He shows his clients how to cook healthy versions of their favourite dishes (like a Subway meatball melt, chicken tikka masala, beef and ale pie, lasagne, beef ragu and loads more – my favourite is the chicken, cheese and chorizo!) – and most of them take just 15 minutes, and can be cooked using one pan – making the clean-up super easy too.

He then advises doing HIIT training between three and five times a week – with each session taking just 10 to 15 minutes. As Joe himself says – "Eat more. Exercise less.".

I used to drive for 20 minutes to go to the gym, spend an hour on the treadmill, or the bike, and then drive another 20 minutes home. With showering, changing etc., one exercise session took a good two hours out of my day.

Doing a HIIT session from home means I can leave my desk, do a HIIT session, have a shower, and be back at my desk, all within 20 to 25 minutes – saving me anything up to 90 minutes per training session.

Not only that, but I'm actually seeing BETTER results from the HIIT training than I was from plodding along on the treadmill for an hour – just like Dorian Yates, just like Joe Wicks, I'm finding it more effective – better results from less effort. What's not to like?

Where were all the morbidly obese cavemen?

It's not just sheer luck that this works either – there's actual science behind it. Back when we were all cavemen (and women!), we never used to jog on treadmills for an hour at a time. We'd walk at a fairly sedate pace when we travelled from community to community, not really expending much energy at all. Then suddenly, we'd be faced with a sabre-toothed tiger, and we'd spend the next few minutes sprinting at a really high intensity, almost as if our lives depended on it (because they did!).

Then, we'd capture some food and have to carry a 300-pound animal half a mile back to our village – weight-lifting at a really high intensity, but in intervals!

You don't see many morbidly obese cavemen now, do you?

In 2016, a university in Denmark commissioned a trial of "interval walking" with a group of Type 2 diabetics. They were split into three groups:

1. A control group, who did no exercise

2. A continuous training group, who walked at normal pace for 60 minutes, three times a week

3. An interval training group, who also walked for 60 minutes, three times a week, but who were asked to walk at 70% of their normal walking speed for five minutes, then to walk at 150% of their normal walking speed for one minute, and then repeat the sequence

The control group saw no change to any of their health or diabetes markers.

The continuous training group saw a mild improvement to their glycaemic control and good overall weight loss.

The interval training group saw massive improvements in ALL measured elements. Their glycaemic control was better. Their cholesterol was lower. Their HbA1c tests were improved. They lost more weight. Their body fat percentages dropped. They were happier, and when surveyed said that they were more likely to continue with the training than the other two groups.

The interesting thing with this study is that they didn't actually work any harder than the "continuous training" group – because they rested between intervals, they ended up walking the same distance, over the same time period, expending the same energy. Yet working in intervals made the exercise much more effective.

Do you want to know the good news?

Interval training works in business too.

"Is the building on fire, Pete?"

One of my mentors used to tell anyone who'd listen how he'd built his empire in 90-minute chunks. He identified that the very start of the working day was when he was at his best – when he had the most energy, when his creative juices were flowing at high tide, and he was able to achieve amazing things given just an hour and a half of uninterrupted, focused, high-intensity work per day.

Note that he wasn't just "working hard" for 90 minutes. He's working at 100%, on the RIGHT things (see chapter six – I blame Richard Branson – to help you choose the right things for you!), and he's working in a place that some might call "flow". Others might refer to it as "the zone".

He's created an environment that is conducive to him achieving more in those first 90 minutes of one day than most people achieve given eight hours.

Often he would be the first person in the office, sometimes opening up at 6:30am, just so he could ensure being left alone in "the zone" for those 90 minutes before the staff start filing in. If the phone rang in the office, he didn't answer it. His own mobile phone was turned off. His email was shut down. He was there to focus on ONE THING, and ONE THING ONLY.

In the early days, he suffered some interruptions from well-meaning members of staff, who wanted to speak to him about something happening later in the day, to get a signature, or just his thoughts about something. He tried telling them that he wasn't to be disturbed, but time and again, someone would come in and interrupt his flow.

Eventually, he got a sign made for his office door: "Do not interrupt unless building is on fire."

It didn't take long to train the staff either...

Knock! Knock!

"Morning boss, can I just..."

"Is the building on fire, Pete?"

"Err, no boss, it's just that."

"F*** off then."

Once he's done his ONE THING, then the door is open, and Pete is free to go in. But Pete now knows, when the door's shut, and the Boss is working on his ONE THING, you do NOT interrupt!

Should I even be DOING this?

Anyone who says they "haven't got time" to grow their business, start building up their network, or learning a new skill probably has poor time management skills. They're probably looking at cat videos on Facebook right now.

By the way, if Facebook is a massive time vampire for you – sucking hours out of your day, I can highly recommend downloading a "news feed blocker" plugin for your internet browser – it's a tidy piece of code that means you can use the productive parts of Facebook that you MIGHT want to use to grow your business – groups, messenger, notifications etc.

But the minute you click on the logo to go to your news feed and get that little hit of dopamine as you catch up on the political views of someone you went to school with 20 years ago, and watching how to make Cadbury's Creme Egg brownies (I'm hungry just REMEMBER-ING that video), instead of your usual news feed, you get...

Nothing.

Just a blank page.

You can go back to the productive parts of Facebook. Or you can bug-ger off back to what you SHOULD be doing. What you can't do is waste the next hour scrolling and liking, scrolling and liking. No word of a lie, I reckon this free news feed blocker has saved me hundreds of "lost" hours per year.

If it's not Facebook, then what else are you wasting your time on? Per-form a time audit, and find out – set a timer to go off every 15 minutes (during working hours!) for one week. When the timer goes off, just jot down (in a few words) what you've been doing for the last 15 minutes.

This doesn't need to take you more than 10 seconds – just note down "emails" or "phone calls", "staff meeting" or "sales presentation". Then after a week, you can see exactly how much time you've spent getting and keeping new customers, and how much time you've spent "check-ing email".

Once you've got that complete list of everything that you do, work through and ask yourself two questions for each "thing" that you do –

1. Why am I doing this?
2. Could someone else (other than me!) do this?

The important/urgent matrix

You need to know that you are investing your time intelligently, in the areas and tasks that will actually take you towards your goals at the fastest possible pace. I like to use the important/urgent matrix to help me decide what to work on:

Is it...	Urgent?	Not urgent?
Important?	1	2
Not important?	3	4

1. Urgent and important. These are things that have to be done NOW, that either could not have been foreseen, or you've left until the last minute (urgent), but they also take you towards your goal (important). I aim to spend around 20% of my time working here.

2. Not urgent, but important. There's no upcoming deadline for these tasks, but they are the things that will propel your business forward. I spend 70% to 80% of my time working on tasks that fall into this section – writing sales copy, recording videos and podcasts, managing investments, etc.

3. Urgent, but not important. These tasks get delegated to someone else.

4. Not urgent, and not important. Don't touch anything here with a barge pole! It's fine to dip into this section every now and then to "check emails" – and then filter them into sections 1, 2 or 3. But so many people I speak to spend half their working day sat in section 4, keeping "busy", but achieving nothing.

 BIG IDEA...
Stop being "busy", start being EFFECTIVE.

Rest is as important as work

I really wish I'd discovered the power of working in intervals years ago – I used to plod along, working at about 70% for over 100 hours every week. I'd end the week shattered, physically and mentally drained, and I'd barely dragged my business forward more than one or two inches.

Now I work at 100% for around an hour a day. Sometimes it's less, and sometimes it's more – but 90 minutes is about the limit that I'm able to sustain a 100% interval. That enables me to coast at 50% for the rest of the day. If you happen to pass by my office when I'm working at 50%, you'd probably ponder to yourself how the hell I achieve anything in my business, as I seem laid back, unhurried, and unstressed.

You'd probably call me lazy if you caught me during a 50% phase.

But I need to coast at 50% for a reason. As Dorian Yates figured out, you HAVE to have the rest periods to make the intervals effective. If I was to do 90 minutes at 100%, and then try and maintain 70% or 80% for the rest of the day, I'd be knackered by mid-afternoon, and crucially, I'd be less effective.

Kind of like Joe Wicks' mantra, but I'll amend it to "Work less. Relax more."

I'm still expending the same level of energy doing 100% / 50% intervals, as I would be working the whole day at 70%, only I achieve more.

Plus I get the power of momentum swinging in my favour too – working at 100% for that first hour or so of the day, to really FOCUS on that ONE THING that truly matters, to work uninterrupted on it, and to get into flow, into the zone, means that by 10am most mornings, I've already achieved the most important thing that I needed to do that day – I've won the day.

Even if I achieve nothing else for the remainder of the day, if I waste every single moment on minutiae, if I spend my Mondays watching cat videos on Facebook, or my Thursdays playing "video roulette" on YouTube, I can still chalk that day up in the "win" column – because I blocked out the time for that first hour or two, and dedicated it to working at 100% on my ONE THING.

The 100% test

You need to know what 100% looks like. You may think that you already know what it looks like, but I'd hazard a guess that what most people think is 100% is actually 80% to 90%.

Try this exercise.

Put both your arms up above your head. Your left hand should be about 30 centimetres above your left ear, and your right hand should be as high as you can reach it.

Now raise your right hand two inches.

If you managed to raise your right hand two inches, then guess what? You weren't working at 100% when I told you to put it "as high as you can reach it" just now!

You may need to consciously force yourself to focus 100% on the task in hand the first few times, but eventually, you'll develop a "radar" for this, and you'll know whether you're giving it 100% or not – you're either in the zone, or you're not. There is no in between.

 BIG IDEA...

What does 100% look like for YOU?

"But I really struggle with focus. There's no way I can work at 100% for an hour or more!" If that sounds like you, then try working in smaller intervals! Instead of a single 60-90 minute interval, try working at 100% for 15 minutes, then take a five-minute break, and do another 15 minutes at 100% and rest again for five minutes.

Repeat that cycle four times, and you've just done an hour of focused work on your ONE THING.

It doesn't matter whether you want to lose weight, win Mr Olympia, write a best-selling book, win the big contract, or build a million pound business. Nothing beats working at a high intensity for short periods – this HIIT works.

Anyone for some steamed midget-trees?

WHICH END OF THE SEE-SAW DO YOU WANT TO SIT?

"Work is a rubber ball. If you drop it, it will bounce back. The other four balls – family, health, friends, integrity – are made of glass. If you drop one of these, it will be irrevocably scuffed, nicked, perhaps even shattered."

Gary Keller

Ah, "work / life balance" – that old chestnut. The holy grail of the working family man or woman for generations.

I've already mentioned my desire NOT to end up like the poster boys of British Entrepreneurship, Messrs Branson and Sugar, guys who built billion-pound businesses whilst their kids had to read the newspaper or turn on the TV if they wanted to spend some time with their dad. Before I had kids, I really didn't give a toss about "work / life balance" – my work WAS my life. And it wasn't like I had kids to think about then, so it's all about earning a crust, right?

Well, apart from the fact it totally screwed up my health to the point that, when I look back at photos of me from that time (around 10 years ago), I look at least 10 years older than I do NOW! As for relationships with friends and family? Not a chance. Work came first, second and third.

I now liken the whole "work / life balance" thing to a see-saw, with "work" at one end, and "life" at the other. Sit in the exact centre, and you'll get balance. But you won't have much fun, and it doesn't really achieve anything.

Go and put all your weight behind the "work" end, and you'll see great results there. The more effort you put into pushing and pulling the "work" end, the more momentum you'll get, and you'll have work totally under your control.

The other end though, the "life" end, will be completely out of control – if your newborn baby was sat on the "life" end when you leapt, full-blooded on the "work" end, he or she is probably a couple of miles away by now, having just begun their descent...

Similarly, if you spend all your time at the "life" end, it will be work that suffers.

See-saws work better with two

See-saws need at least two people to work properly. So does achieving a work / life balance.

You're going to need others around you – either to take the slack and keep the business growing whilst you're at the "life" end of the see-saw, or supportive family members, partners, or childcare etc. to keep things running whilst you're off growing your empire.

Either way, you need someone else counter-balancing your weight whilst you're at either end of the see-saw. And you need to make sure that you spread your time over BOTH ends – otherwise, you're not getting that balance, are you?

What most people try and do, is sit at both ends themselves – they'll be "spending time with the kids" whilst actually checking emails on their phone. They'll "just nip into the office" on their day off, or "just get the laptop out for an hour whilst we watch TV". If you've ever tried having a conversation with your partner when they're buried nose-deep in their phone, you'll know how effective this is!

 BIG IDEA...

Be 100% PRESENT, whether at work or play.

For me, the key is to be 100% in "work" mode, or 100% in "life" mode. And then have VERY clear, strict boundaries between the two.

When I'm planning my week, I'll block out chunks of time, to fit in the important stuff from BOTH "work" and "life" – things like:

- School runs
- Spending time with kids after school
- Recording podcast
- Meeting with financial director
- Date night with 'Er Indoors
- Mentoring meeting
- Gym time
- Plan marketing campaign

Those are ALL protected. When I'm spending time with the kids after school, that's ALL I'm doing. I'm 100% present for them. I don't answer my phone during this time, and I don't check emails or dick about on Facebook. That's only possible because I have the "second person" – a great team, who I can trust to run my business for an hour or two whilst I live my life.

BIG IDEA...

Block out time for the important things that AREN'T work too.

Then, when I'm in the middle of planning a huge marketing campaign, I'm 100% in work mode – the kids are either at school, or there's another "second person" looking after THEM whilst I'm taking care of things at the other end of the see-saw.

I have blocks of protected time for the important stuff, from BOTH ends of the see-saw.

Be 100% there, no matter which end you're at.

Clearly defined boundaries.

Don't let other people tell you which end to sit at

One of the keys to achieving "balance" is to know when you're out of balance. Most people know instinctively when they've been neglecting their family or their work, but sometimes it needs an intervention

– and sometimes YOU'RE the one who needs to give yourself that intervention.

That's what I did, but it took the shock of that Alan Sugar quote for me to REALISE that I was so far out of balance, that what I THOUGHT I desired (a huge global brand, with hundreds of staff and offices in sky-scrapers all over the world), was actually nothing like what I truly desired (an ambitious lifestyle business).

I'd always seen "lifestyle businesses" decried by the likes of that lanky prat with the pinstripe suit on Dragons' Den, who always looked down his nose at people who didn't fit his criteria of what a "real business" is. And it was a chance conversation with one of the former Dragons, Doug Richard, that changed my mind.

He implored me to believe in lifestyle businesses – he made the point that the success of a business (or failure) is determined by its bottom line (profit), NOT its top line (turnover). It's determined by the quality of life it delivers to the owner, not by the number of people it employs. He got fed up listening to pitch after pitch whereby it seemed that the sole purpose of a "proper business" was to raise enough VC money to make it to the next round of funding, where you could borrow yet more money.

There are very few other people that get congratulated by all their peers for getting millions of pounds into debt, without having to worry about delivering profit.

That's when I discovered what I TRULY desired.

An ambitious lifestyle business.

Yes, I want to earn good money. I am ambitious – I think big, and I want a business that delivers the best lifestyle for me. Some have tried to talk me into taking VC money in the past, but that is completely treasonous to the "job description" that I wrote for myself, as CEO of this new ambitious lifestyle business:

"To do what I want, where I want, how I want, when I want, if I want..."

Getting EVERYONE sat on the see-saw

We've even written the "ambitious lifestyle company" element into our staff's contracts.

we make it very clear that we want them to ENJOY working for us – and that means enjoying their life.

If you can get your work done in two hours in the morning and you want to go to the beach in the afternoon, crack on. Go for it.

You want to sleep all day and build code through the night? Why not! You want to work around school runs or play golf with your grand-dad? Sure thing.

As long as you remember that we're an ambitious lifestyle business so it's not all about the lifestyle. We are also ambitious and we are a business. We are here to make money.

Everyone works from home. We've got no set hours or fixed office. You haven't got to do a nine to five chained to a desk.

All of my team members work flexible hours to suit their lifestyle, but when the shit hits the fan or we're in the middle of a huge marketing campaign it's payback time, and it's kind of, "Right, everybody, you need to come down THIS end of the see-saw now."

We're now down the business / work end. It is now all hands to the pump. 100 hour weeks are back on, but you maybe do a 100 hour week twice a year when we've got a massive campaign on.

The rest of the time, if you can get your work done in 20 hours a week, give me 20 hours a week.

It hasn't been for everyone, and we've had to let several people go who just didn't fit with the ambitious lifestyle business ethos – given a little freedom, some people took the piss, and thought they didn't need to work at ALL! But we're in a much better place having "kissed a few frogs", and now have a small team of really happy team players, who step up when we need them to, and who know that we're there for THEM when they need us.

Sometimes, as employers, you need to let your staff spend some time at the other end of the see-saw. Because when you do that, they'll (normally) repay you by putting ever more oomph in when they get back on the "work" end.

Which end of the see-saw have you spent most of the last week at?

THERE'S NO "I" IN "TEAM"
(BUT THERE ARE FIVE IN "INDIVIDUAL BRILLIANCE"...)

Journalist: "How many people work at the Vatican, Your Excellency?"

Pope John Paul II: "About half of them."

What does 100% look like?

I'm writing this chapter sat in a hotel room in Bristol at the moment, having spent the day with my mastermind group.

A familiar topic came up, as it did in one of our One Percent Club meetings last night..."Bloody staff not doing what they're told".

In almost every situation where we come across this, the problem lies not just with the "bloody staff member", but with the business owner's communication processes (or lack thereof).

This is a lesson that Sir Alex Ferguson (who certainly knows a thing or two about putting together winning teams, and absolutely wouldn't stand for anyone not towing the line) can teach us well.

All he did with his teams was set the expectations for each individual REALLY high – and then let them know what that expectation was.

"That's what 100% looks like" he would tell them.

Then, if a player fell short of the agreed expectation, he'd let them know – "THIS is 100%. You've given me 90%. I want 100%."

If it happened again?

Out came "the hairdryer" speech – to remind them in no uncertain terms what 100% looks like, and that 100% is what's expected.

But what if they keep on doing it?

They go.

Doesn't matter if they're your star striker, club captain, or the chairman's son – you're out.

We only have people in our team who give 100% every time.

What does 100% look like in your business?

Do your team members know what 100% looks like for them?

Are they giving you 100% every time?

Are YOU giving them everything THEY need to give you 100%?

Never hire your mates. I did once, but I think I got away with it

I realised quite early on in my business career that I couldn't do it all myself. Whilst I was earning really good money compared to what I had been taking home from the Civil Service, I was also working pretty much every hour of every day and physically couldn't do anymore. Yet I knew that if I wrote more content, created more web pages, got more marketing out there, added more customers to my mailing list and sent them more emails, there was even more money to be made.

I could only work as hard as one person.

In the early days, when you're bootstrapping, it makes perfect sense to try and do everything yourself. But as you grow, it makes less and less sense to be a "jack-of-all-trades, master-of-none". You need to stop thinking that "no-one can do it better than me."

 BIG IDEA...

STOP trying to do it all YOURSELF.

So I made my very first hire, which went against everything that I would do now – and I hired a mate of mine. He was someone who was a friend, who I enjoyed spending time with at the pub, someone who had zero experience in internet marketing (compared to my 15 months of doing this full time), but who was a good laugh, and who was looking for a new job.

And so it was that Jason Brockman started working for me on April Fool's Day, 2003.

Unbelievably, it worked out. As employee #1, Jason is not only still with me today, 14 years later, but he's now also my business partner. We've gone into several ventures together, and we seem to complement each other perfectly. Jason builds robust systems and processes, making sure the customer journey works as well as it should, and that everything that SHOULD happen, does happen. Which leaves me free to focus on sales and marketing – or to put it another way, to try and break those systems and processes by throwing as many customers as possible at them!

 BIG IDEA...

Find a business partner who COMPLETES you, not competes with you.

He's the Yin to my Yang, the Morecambe to my Wise, the Ant to my Dec, the Hinge to my Bracket, the Barry Chuckle to my Paul Chuckle. We're often on the same wavelength, but we do think very differently, and we have completely different skill sets, so it's very rare that we step on one another's toes. We trust each other well enough because we know that the other is better at what they do than we are – and vice versa.

If you have two business partners who both see themselves as the expert in sales and marketing, then it's likely they'll be squabbling over every marketing campaign and every sales opportunity. Meanwhile, who's putting those robust systems and processes in place? Who's looking after the numbers? Who's leading the staff? Who's going to look after the admin, and who's going to sweep the floor and lock up at night?

No-one, I expect, because neither of the partners wants to do that – they want to focus on their strengths. Unfortunately, their strengths lie in the same areas, and so the business suffers. That's why Jason and I work together so well – I can trust him to work to his strengths, he can trust me to work to mine, and our businesses thrive as a result.

Oh, and we're still mates too.

Elon Musk isn't hanging around the jobcentre

Whilst it's worked out well for me (on that one occasion!), hiring one of your mates to do a job they've never done before isn't the best bit of advice I could give you. I think we can chalk the fact that it worked out so brilliantly up to luck rather than judgement.

 BIG IDEA...

NEVER hire friends or family.

Hindsight has proven this to be the case, as whilst employee #1 is still with us to this day, employees number 2, 3, 4, 5, 6, 7, 9, 10, 11, 12, 14 and 17 are not.

Whilst we didn't exactly continue hiring our mates, we did hire people based on whether we LIKED them, and then we treated them more as mates than employees. That means that we hired some pretty poor people, and MANAGED them even worse. They were left to their own devices, weren't given any direction, and I expected them all to be entrepreneurial like me – "There's your desk. Go earn some money!"

Of course, there was one major flaw with that plan – they weren't entrepreneurial in the slightest. They were employees, who wanted a job. They wanted to be given a clearly defined role, one that would challenge and motivate them, one that they could walk out of the door at 5pm and leave behind. And that's the way it should be. If you had a team full of Type A entrepreneurs, everyone would want to do the sales pitch, and write the marketing strategy, but the filing wouldn't get done, and the floors wouldn't get swept. If you surround yourself with people like you, then no-one will want to do the grunt work – and that probably means YOU'LL end up doing it!

You don't find entrepreneurs at the jobcentre. If you advertise at the job centre, you'll find people looking for jobs. I know that now, but remember – I'd worked at the job centre myself. That's how I found a job. And I think like an entrepreneur. But I was the EXCEPTION rather than the rule. The next Richard Branson or Elon Musk probably isn't hanging around the job centre. The people who ARE hanging around the job centre are those who are struggling to find work (i.e. those that the jobs market doesn't want), and those who have no intention of finding work, but have been told to hang around the job centre so they can get their benefits.

Neither of these types of people are going to be the ones you need to drive your business forward.

The amazing staff snowball

If you're one person, you can only work as hard as one person. When you have a team, that gives you leverage. Having an AMAZING team gives you HUGE leverage.

The difference between an "average" member of staff and an awesome one might mean paying them 20% or 30% more, but the ROI (return on investment) difference could be 500% or 600%, and that's just on ONE member of staff.

Multiply that ROI by a team of five, six or seven, and you can see how we currently achieve so much, even with a relatively small team.

Then, (and this is where the fun REALLY starts) summon your inner Warren Buffett, and whip out your compound interest calculator (What do you mean, you don't have one? Just Google "compound interest calculator"), and compound the hell out of that massively increased ROI for ten years or more.

An average team of five could turn a £50,000 per year business into a £1,000,000 per year business in ten years.

An AMAZING team of five could turn a £50,000 per year business into a business that employs ten people and generates profits in excess of £1,500,000 per year in ten years.

Most people overestimate what they can achieve in one year, and massively underestimate what they can achieve given a decade. The numbers don't lie though – replacing an "average" member of staff – someone who "does the job" (that's about it), with someone who absolutely knocks it out of the park most days, results in a business that is FIFTEEN times the size it otherwise would be after ten years.

Sure, those kick-ass members of staff will cost you 20% to 30% more, be harder to find, and it means you can't just employ your friends and family. But look again at those numbers... What do you want to show for ten years' hard work growing a business – 100% growth, or 2,900% growth?

Do you want to work with staff who do the bare minimum, spend their days clock-watching, somehow forget to do the boring tasks they hate, but never forget when they're "due" a pay-rise (or a "civil servant" as we call them...)?

Or do you want to work with staff who are the BEST at what they do, who LOVE what they do, who fit into the business like a glove? Who reduce the pressure on you as the business owner, who require less day-to-day management, who will actually EARN their next pay rise?

I've hired both – and I know which I prefer. Ask me again in ten years, and I reckon I'll be 2,900% more convinced...

Lessons from a Mickey Mouse operation

If you've ever been to Walt Disney World in Florida, you'll no doubt have been amazed by the sheer size of it. The thing that really hit me was the sheer size of the organisation in terms of the people. At the time of writing, Disney employs something like 195,000 people – that's almost the size of the population of my home city (Plymouth)!

Whilst you're in one of the Disney parks, everything appears "magical", the employees all just seem to love what they do, and enjoy creating these wonderful memories for their visitors. That doesn't just happen by accident. Every Disney employee (or "cast member" as they're referred to) is trained extensively in "the Disney way". They're given a huge list of scenarios and told EXACTLY how to react in each one. If A happens, do this. If B happens, do that. If A, B and C all happen at the same time, do this.

We saw it time and time again – things just worked as clockwork. A cast member would be checking people in for the rides, and if they found themselves talking to a guest for longer than 15 seconds, a second cast member would appear, as if from nowhere, and take over the role that the first cast member was originally performing. Then they'd vanish back to whatever they were doing before.

It's Disney policy that cast members are to go out of their way to make sure that your visit is practically perfect, and unlike many such claims in this country, they're not just paying it lip service. Cast members are given full autonomy to do and say whatever they want to make your day "magical" – and we saw several examples of this, from a princess who was happy to break character and talk Star Wars with our eldest, to a cast member who was able to help us track down a character that we wanted to meet – in a totally different park.

BIG IDEA...

Give your team STRICT guidelines on your company ethos, and the FREEDOM to interpret it themselves.

The only thing they're NOT allowed to say is "I don't know". If you ask where the nearest restroom is, they're supposed to actually walk you there, not just point in the general direction. And if you want to know what Olaf eats for breakfast, or whether Captain Hook has a girlfriend, just ask a cast member, and they'll come up with an answer pretty damn quick.

Whilst they're given autonomy, it's within a strict hierarchy. I read an interview with a former cast member who said "Everything said by attractions hosts? Scripted. Everything said by performers on the streets in the parks? Scripted. Many things said by retail hosts? Scripted. We're given every last piece of information about our attraction so that we can ALWAYS stay on script."

You'll never see a cast member point with one finger – that could be interpreted as rude, so they'll only ever point with two fingers. All cast members are responsible for keeping the park tidy – walking past some litter on the ground is a disciplinary matter, as is bringing chewing gum into the park. Cast members are even given instructions on

HOW to pick up litter – they're not supposed to stop and pick it up, but to bend as they walk past and scoop it up.

It's an amazing setup, because it's so rigid in its "how-to" handbook for staff, whilst also giving them the autonomy they need to live up to Walt's core values. But it's that discipline of the detail – "This is how you point. This is how you pick up litter. This is what you say when A happens. This how you react when B happens" – that gives cast members the freedom to know EXACTLY what "the Disney way" is – and to react and behave accordingly in ANY situation.

We saw one or two examples of cast members who, for whatever reason didn't fit in. That's natural in an organisation with 195,000 people working for you, and whilst they weren't doing anything that you or I would consider "bad", they just stood out as "not acting in the Disney way" – saying the line "Have a magical day" whilst your face is saying "I'm bored out of my brain" for example – but I wouldn't mind betting that those cast members are no longer employed by Disney, because if I can spot them standing out like a sore thumb after a couple of weeks in the parks, you can bet your arse that Disney management can spot them a mile off, and they'll be out of the door before Mickey's had a chance to say "See you real soon".

"I'm sorry, we're going to have to let you go"

If you're starting to have thoughts about firing one or two of your team, then that's usually the point at which you probably should have ALREADY let them go. I think the quickest we've ever fired someone was two months after they started, but I've known of people who have fired people on their FIRST DAY – you've got to have a seriously bad attitude (or partake in some serious gross misconduct) to get the boot on your very first day – but I've seen it happen!

What I've seen happen a LOT more often though is business owners hoping that "things will improve", that somehow the member of staff who's been pretty crap for the last five years is suddenly going to turn into the model employee overnight. I'm still waiting for that particular miracle to materialise!

Most people are too slow to hire because they're afraid they'll get a bad one. And those same people are then too slow to FIRE too because they're afraid that they won't be able to get a good one (and I think crucially, they want to avoid confrontation).

"Hire slow, fire fast" is the standard line trotted out when it comes to hiring and firing staff – I prefer to hire fast, and fire fast. I want to get a team in place as soon as possible so that I can leverage my time IMMEDIATELY, and if that person isn't the best person for the job, I want them out of that role as soon as possible so that I can replace them with someone better. The longer I delay doing this, the lower the returns I get from compounding my investment in the team. (Yes, I'm digging out my compound interest calculator again!)

 BIG IDEA...

Hire FAST, fire FAST.

But isn't firing someone really scary? Aren't we going to end up having a slanging match, or might I get punched in the face?

It's never a nice thing to have to do, but scary? It's just another example (see "Telling Fear to F*** Off" for more) of the anticipation being scarier than the actual act.

The minute you've uttered the words "I'm sorry, we're going to have to let you go", you've done the hard part – you've jumped out of the aeroplane, and there's no way back.

Here are just some of the responses I've had when I've said those words:

"Yeah, I thought you were going to say that."

"I half expected you to sack me six months ago!"

"That's cool – I wanted to leave, but didn't want to let you down."

I've never been punched in the face though, and the most common response I've received has NOT been one of anger or confrontation – but one of sadness, quiet contemplation, and of regret that it hasn't worked out. Unless they really ARE deluded (and yes, we've employed one or two of them in our time!), it's unlikely to be a total surprise to them that things haven't exactly been going well, but most people don't like to admit that they're not capable of doing a job – they'd rather wait and be sacked first. See, it's not just small business owners that avoid confrontation!

That being said, they probably didn't wake up that morning and expect to be coming home with a box full of their possessions and their P45, so there IS the potential to get into a slanging match over "so-and-so should have been sacked before me", or "I know how to do my job better than you", or any of the "he said/she said" debate. You want to avoid this at all costs. Stick to the facts.

We're letting you go. Here's a letter that explains our decision. Your notice period is X days. You have X days of unused holiday pay remaining. You are no longer required to work as of right now – your notice period will be paid in lieu.

If you're concerned at any level about whether you CAN legally fire someone, always consult a HR professional. I can recommend Jacqui Mann from J Mann Associates (www.jmassociates.org).

They'll have a quick chat with you to find out what's going on, and let you know where you stand; they also offer a range of services, from templated termination letters, to more hands-on HR help.

 BIG IDEA...
Run dismissals past a HR expert first.

Attitude over aptitude – hire a good hurdler

When hiring now, I'm always on the look-out for a really good attitude over aptitude. Whilst I do like to follow the traditional advice to hire people who are better than me, I don't want to hire someone who knows it all – or at least THINKS that they do! If they've got the right attitude, then we can always train the aptitude, and teach the rest.

How do you test for attitude? One thing we've done is to put hurdles in place for those members of staff that you THINK would be good at what they do. Because of where we're based, in deepest, darkest Devon (and the fact that all of our team work remotely, from home), we've quite often used distance as one of those hurdles. Joe, our horse racing tipster, lives in Norwich. I interviewed him in Birmingham, which is about a three-hour drive for him. He got there at his own expense, and even stayed in a hotel overnight, again at his own expense – which was a clear indicator of the right attitude.

 BIG IDEA...

Hire for ATTITUDE, not aptitude. You can always train the skills, attitude is ingrained.

If the first question a potential interviewee asks is "Do I get paid bus fare for coming to the interview?", that's a red flag that they could be a right PITA, and is certainly NOT the attitude we're looking for.

We've interviewed someone from Essex, 136 miles away in Cheltenham, and dragged another person 237 miles from London to our base in Plymouth for an interview.

If someone's willing to complete a near 500-mile round trip for the POSSIBILITY of a job, then that's a really good indicator that they've got the kind of attitude we're looking for, and that the role we've advertised really appeals to them.

What other hurdles could you put in their way? Try sneaking some "out of the ordinary" instructions into the application instructions – "For guaranteed instant rejection, send a boring, bog-standard CV to cv@mybusiness.co.uk, otherwise, please dazzle us with a two-minute video which shows us why you'd be perfect for this role."

Or ask them to work for free for a day. Or a week. This isn't about getting free labour, it's all about their REACTION to being asked to work without reward. Watch their expression change as you ask them to give up their time for free, so that you can make a decision based on seeing them "in the role" – asking someone to do something without the instant gratification of pay for work done is a HUGE test of character, and if you've got someone who doesn't hesitate, and happily gives up a day (or a week) to show you what they're capable of, you know you've got a good one – someone who plays the long game.

Don't stick your star striker in goal

So, we've fired all of our "bad apples" replaced them with superstars – all we need to do now is sit back and wait for the compound growth, right?

Well, not quite. As any Man City fan will tell you, just putting a team of random superstars together and expecting them to win the league just doesn't work. You've got to have the right superstars in the right place, and they need to be properly trained, managed, coached, and looked after.

Every business should have an organisation chart – a flowchart that shows the company structure and hierarchy. You need to know who does what, and who answers to whom. You may want to delegate everything you possibly can, but you still need to hold people accountable. The company org chart should have a degree of responsibility running through it.

The entry-level staff report to the team leaders. Team leaders report to management. Management reports to the shareholders. But every single role within the company has a place on the org chart, so you can see how the flow of responsibility runs through the company, and if something goes wrong, you know exactly whose responsibility it is to fix.

See: www.smartdraw.com/organizational-chart/examples for some example of org charts that you could adapt for your own business. Don't be put off by thinking you don't need an org chart because you work on your own, or you've only got a small team – all of these roles still need filling – even if it's your name that you're putting next to each role within the organisation.

When I first started out, I was head of marketing, bookkeeper, web designer, copywriter, payroll (admittedly it was an easy job – with only me to pay!), managing director, tea boy, customer service department, salesman, admin assistant and chief pot washer – and that was just ONE morning's work.

BIG IDEA...

EVERY business should have an ORG CHART, even if you're a one-man band.

But then as I grew, I was able to delegate some of those roles and responsibilities, and suddenly, other people's names started to appear on my org chart, as I found someone who specialised in bookkeeping, another who loves admin, and one who writes amazing copy. We've got a web designer who can actually write code, and someone working in sales who loves nothing more than picking up the phone and closing deals. As I write this now, my org chart has 27 different roles on it – and my name is only next to three of them – shareholder, MD, and marketing director.

If I wanted to completely remove myself from the business, I would need to hire an MD and a marketing director. I would then have my name next to just one role within the organisation – that of the shareholder. Thanks to the org chart, I'll be able to sleep well at night knowing the business is in safe hands without me due to the degree of responsibility running through the organisation. The staff at the bottom of the chart report to their team leaders. The team leaders report to the board of directors. The board of directors answers to the MD. And the MD reports directly to me.

KPIs help you keep score

For this to work though, you need to have key performance indicators (KPIs) running throughout the company – every single member of staff needs to know what THEIR KPIs are, and how their job affects them. Everyone must OWN their KPIs. The KPI report is how the team leaders know their staff are on track. It's how the board of directors knows the team leaders are being effective. It's how the MD knows his (or her) board of directors is working to their capabilities, and it's how

I, as the shareholder of the company, know that my MD is doing what I ask of him / her and that my company is in safe hands.

Every month, my team puts together a KPI report for the previous month. This tells us how we're performing against a "usual" month, how many leads we're getting, where we're getting them from, how much we're paying for them, how many are converting into sales for each product, and what marketing channels are driving those sales. The customer service team allows me to have an "ear to the ground" on what our customers are saying – positive and negative. This data is crucial to me if I want to grow the business, to make it more effective, but crucially, it's not about the team just blindly handing me some stats once a month – they own those KPIs, they want to improve on the numbers. They KNOW what level they should be hitting.

And the minute they start failing to hit those numbers, when the KPIs start dropping, I know about it – and can react immediately, whether that's diverting marketing resources away from a campaign or traffic source that is performing poorly, training (or retraining) staff, fixing a part of a system or process that has broken, or changing our strategy entirely. No longer will I wait until I'm feeling the effects of those elements in terms of less cash coming into the bank – no, I want to react NOW and keep that flow of cash coming in.

Are your customer satisfaction survey results dropping below a certain level? Phones being answered after four rather than three rings? Is EVERY customer offered the upsell? How many times does the sales team follow up?

What are the KPIs in YOUR business? Who's going to OWN them? And how do you MONITOR them?

 BIG IDEA...

What KPIs do YOU need to know?

My team doesn't see the monthly KPI report as a chore, as just another report they spend hours churning out for management, never to see any feedback from it. I go through the report in detail with Jason, but also with the team members individually – and I react to it. If our customer service team tells me there's a problem with X, I'll speak to them about ways we can address it. And I WILL address it. Once again, just "DOING what you said you're going to do" wins the day.

What does your team want from you?

Communication with your team should be two-way. I see far too many bosses thinking that barking orders at their staff is going to deliver them the business they want. It might work for some people, but it's not MY style, and it's not most people's either. If you're going to attract real superstars to come and work for you (and want to stand any chance in hell of keeping them), they're going to want to ENJOY working for you.

They're going to want some autonomy. They want to feel trusted, respected, that you believe in them – so give them the opportunity to earn that trust and respect, the chance to showcase what they can do. Give them their own set of KPIs, and the autonomy to use their skillset in the best way they see fit to hit, and ultimately, grow those KPIs.

Don't interpret "autonomy" as saying to someone on their first day "There's your desk. Don't bother me again. See you in 12 months for your annual appraisal". I don't even have annual appraisals with my team – we'll sit down a few times a year and talk about the big picture stuff, personal development, etc. But why wait a year to let them know they're doing a great job? Or worse, wait a year to let them know they're NOT doing a good job?

Ditch those formal annual appraisals, and instead meet up once a quarter for a "big picture" chat. Have a 1-2-1 with every team member once a month. Have an energetic team meeting once a week, and a five-minute "team huddle" every day.

Do you know what item employees listed as their most desired "perk" of the job?

No, it wasn't a huge salary. It wasn't a brand new BMW. Pension? Nope! It wasn't even free tea and biscuits.

It was being told "thank you" when they'd done a good job.

To feel that they were listened to. Respected. Trusted.

If the marketing team shows me that there's a marketing channel delivering huge ROIs that we're not currently tapping, guess what? Their marketing budget just increased so they can test some more. I've kept every KPI report since we started doing them, and it's amazing to see the transformation in the business as a result – several times the KPI report has thrown up an underlying issue with the business, long before we would otherwise have spotted it – and it's given us the chance to react, to pivot, to change course – to find continual, never-ending, improvement.

That's what I ask of my team, and bless their cotton socks, they never fail to deliver.

YOU'RE NOT AS GOOD AS YOU THINK YOU ARE...

"Some days you're the Titanic, some days you're the iceberg, and some days you're the guy who jumped off and hit a propeller on the way down."

Jamie Woodham

Mr Midas Touch

As I look back on almost two decades of running small businesses, there are one or two moments when I would have been forgiven for thinking that I had the Midas touch, when literally everything I touched turned to money. The golden age for me was in 2002 and 2003 – I'd literally only just given up the day job a few months earlier, when Google Adwords launched in the UK, and I was there on day one, buying traffic for my freebie website at $0.01 per click.

Google had been completely ads-free until then (I know kids, I know... Take a look on the Wayback Machine website if you don't believe me!), the click-through rates I got were something like 85%. And I was then able to turn that 1 cent visitor into an average of 15 pence – so an instant return of around 2,500% on my investment – not bad!

And of course, that was just one website, and one search term. I discovered the "secret" of SEO (a.k.a. How to rank #1 on Google for most search terms) – buy a domain name with the search terms in it, chuck up a really crappy looking one-page website with the keyword stuffed in there, and link to it from an existing site using the same keyword as the "anchor text" (the words used in the hyperlink).

Rinse. And. Repeat.

Then I started playing around with Adwords some more (well you would, if you were getting a 2,500% return, wouldn't you!), and realised that I didn't even need to OWN the websites I was sending the

Google traffic to – I could just work with the affiliate networks, and get paid a commission for every sale that was tracked to "my" link.

Thanks to Adwords, I could buy any number of highly targeted, extremely relevant web traffic, and send it to merchants who would pay for any sales that were made – win/win!

Before you know it, I had a team of developers working for me, churning out hundreds of thousands of web pages, across 40 or 50 different sectors, all using my "secret" SEO strategy, whilst I focused on building up the Adwords side of the business, sending merchants highly targeted visitors from Google, and getting paid a commission for every sale.

Now, I've always been a lazy bugger, and if there's low-hanging fruit to be had, then I'm going to fill my boots with it – as Warren Buffett says "I prefer finding one-foot hurdles that we can step over, as opposed to developing an ability to leap 7-footers". So as I started playing with Adwords, sending people who were looking for "men's boxer shorts" to a page on M&S selling men's boxer shorts, whilst those who were looking for an "interest free credit card" were directed to somebody like Egg or Capital One, I discovered a source of really relevant keywords, that delivered extraordinary ROIs.

 BIG IDEA...

There's nothing wrong with targeting low-hanging fruit but don't build your FOUNDATIONS on it.

Rather than sending people who were looking for underwear to M&S, I could send people who were searching Google for "M&S" (or "Marks and Spencer", "Marks & Spencer", and all variations thereof) to Marksies, and get paid not just for a few pairs of boxers, but for EVERYTHING that the visitor wanted, from cutlery sets to wedding outfits – and the conversion rate was so high, it was literally a license to print money.

I wasn't the only guy doing this, but I was late to the party, so I had a lot of people to look up to – HGV drivers and factory workers who were now living it up earning over £1m a year; the bloke from Essex who went and moved to a mansion in Portugal; and the guy who shut down his wedding gift list company to focus on Adwords – he ended up on the Sunday Times Rich List eighteen months later.

Clearly, I wasn't the only one with the Midas touch – we were just fellow dotcom millionaires. Guys in their 20s who had an idea, and made it big.

Yep, without a doubt, this was my moment – surely it was only a matter of time before I had to make that big decision – do I host the Apprentice, or become one of the Dragons?

The BBC never called.

Mr Sidam Touch

And just as well, because in 2004 I went from being Mr Midas Touch to the complete opposite – where everything I touched turned to shit. My "secret" SEO strategy that I'd been using to devastating effect was suddenly rendered obsolete with one update of an algorithm by Google, and those stellar returns I was getting from Adwords started getting lower and lower.

Not only were there more rival bidders joining the Adwords gravy train, but Google itself was figuring out what keywords were extremely valuable (so whilst they still let us have "freebies" traffic for $0.10 a click, if I wanted to buy traffic looking for "credit cards" I'd need to be paying $10 a click.

And worst of all, those merchants who I was making an absolute killing from, by sending them Adwords visitors who were searching for their own brand name? Well, they cottoned on to the fact that they could do this themselves, removing the need to pay me at all.

I was merely a middleman, who added no value whatsoever. I was essentially selling them back their own traffic on a commission-only basis, and one-by-one they all added "no brand bidding" to the terms and conditions of their affiliate program.

BIG IDEA...

If you're not adding value, DON'T expect to be in business for long.

Still, that's not too bad – after all, I'm still running a small, nimble enterprise from my spare bedroom, and I've stashed most of this cash that I've been raking in away for a rainy day, haven't I?

Erm, not quite...

Because I thought I was this naturally gifted multi-millionaire, the UK's answer to Donald Trump (back when he was JUST an annoying loud-mouthed businessman), I'd doubled down on my investments, taking on 15 members of staff and a couple of offices, not to mention the obligatory nice big house, foreign holidays and a new car. Oops.

I still had my confidence, of course – so I figured that rather than scaling back to a manageable enterprise, licking my wounds and regrouping, I'd just work harder and harder, on new project after new project. So we launched a competition website. And a bingo site. And a massive portal that was going to do EVERYTHING – it was going to rival Yahoo! in terms of features, with everything from business news and job listings to sports betting odds and the latest weather.

It cost us nearly £150,000 to develop, and never earned us a single penny. We wasted so many man hours building this behemoth of a site, focusing on adding this feature or that feature.

BIG IDEA...

Don't be Kevin Costner. They WON'T come just because you built it.

The one thing we never figured out? How we were actually going to get people to hear about it, let alone use it. That's a huge lesson right there – don't waste time focusing on features, and making everything just perfect – get a minimum viable product out into the marketplace ASAP, and let the marketplace tell YOU whether it's a great idea or not, BEFORE you spend a six-figure sum building something that no-one will ever know about. Kevin Costner syndrome again.

We spent the best part of three years building it, sunk almost £150k into it, and I think I let the domain expire a few years ago, rather than pay the £35 to renew it.

Under my esteemed "leadership", we flitted from one business model to the next – finding something that worked, and trying to scale it up immediately on a grand scale – mainly because I HAD to in order to meet payroll every month now!

I saw a model which was ranking well on Google for some "local" terms – it was a dating website that was set up as a directory, so every local town, village and city in the UK had its own page – something like 60,000 pages in total.

We replicated it, had some success, and immediately set about scaling up, deploying the entire workforce to create these thin, spammy websites which served absolutely no purpose whatsoever, other than to "get in the way" of what people were actually looking for on Google, and send them via one of our affiliate links (or even crazier, to get them to click on one of our Google AdSense ads, which we'd then get a share of).

Before we knew it, we had these directory sites springing up for florists, office space, post offices, takeaways, taxis, restaurants – even sex shops! After four or five months of the entire team working on putting these sites live, they were very NEARLY breaking even.

And then Google moved the goalposts again – completely wiping out all of our rankings for all of the sites.

Back to the drawing board.

At some point we'd set up a shopping directory – it literally listed all the merchants we had an affiliate relationship with; we wrote a few hundred words in the way of a "review", and then plastered our affiliate links all over the page. This was starting to get a little traffic, mainly for brand terms again (people searching for the actual brand names), and was threatening to make a little money.

So once again, the entire team was deployed to scale it up – to go from 100 pages to 2,000 in six months – to really focus on those brand terms, working our SEO "magic" (we also employed some outsourced link builders to get other websites linking to it, which cost us a good few thousand quid!) – and guess what we did?

Yep, we killed it. Not in a "down the kids" killed it kind of way, but in the "zero traffic, zero revenue" way. Once again, we created something that was of zero value to the end user, trying to be the middleman and steal someone else's market share. And once again, Google spotted this a mile off and annihilated us with one tweak of their algorithm.

It seemed at the time that no matter what we did, what we tried, we were destined to fail.

We set up an affiliate management agency, which leaked money like a sieve and struggled to attract clients.

We set up a call centre to provide leads for a life insurance company, and a utility company – the life insurance company screwed us over and didn't pay us, and we lost the contract for the utility company.

We moved out of our offices to save money – and got hit with a £85,000 "repair" bill for work that was SUPPOSED to have been done by our landlord BEFORE we moved in.

Yep, Mr Midas Touch had well and truly left the building by this stage.

Luck happens

But did I actually HAVE the Midas touch back in 2002 / 3? No, of course not – I was simply fortunate enough to be in the right place, at the right time, with the right mindset to be looking for opportunities. Just as I didn't have the Sidam touch (the opposite of the Midas touch) in the years that followed – I was simply making lots of bad decisions, based on a flawed mindset, and those decisions got compounded. I had some bad luck, and I made some bad decisions – that's about it.

Sometimes "luck" happens – good or bad. That doesn't make you a lucky or unlucky person though. I believe that whether you define yourself as "lucky" or "unlucky" depends on which of the two you remember the most. I can certainly say that I've had both very good, and very bad things happen to me that you could attribute to "luck" of one sort or another – but I wouldn't call myself either inherently "lucky" or "unlucky".

BIG IDEA...

"Luck" happens. It's what you DO with it that MATTERS.

Luck happens.

Sometimes you need to recognise that luck has played a part. You've had some success due to good fortune rather than as a result of natural born talent, or you've had some major setbacks due to bad luck – that doesn't mean you're a waste of space. From my experiences, most people will attribute good luck to being gifted, and bad luck to being unlucky – at least publicly.

But privately, it's all too easy to beat yourself up over every little mistake you've made, every failure you've had. We've all got that little voice in our head that moans and nags, and criticises every little thing you do. You say things to yourself that you would never dream of saying out loud to anyone else, and if you dared say some of this "self-talk" to the average person in the street, you'd probably get punched in the face and told where to stick your "advice". It's not helpful in the slightest, we all know that – but it's very, very hard to switch it off.

Talking to yourself again?

Several years ago, I used to struggle a lot with self-confidence. It's taken a couple of years of very deliberate work building that up, doing things that are JUST outside my comfort zone – expanding my hula hoop so to speak. The larger my comfort zone grew, the more self-confidence I was able to find whenever I needed to summon some.

When you do things that are inside your comfort zone, you barely notice the self-talk. That voice in your head is more than happy to let you drift along doing things that it considers "safe", never taking risks or giving people the opportunity to laugh at you. Even when you do things that are only just outside your hula hoop, that voice in your head can be reasoned with – it understands that you probably are capable of doing this, but it'll have a "little chat" with you anyway just to let you know that it expects you're probably going to fail/die/be laughed at/go bankrupt/lose an arm etc., but that you're welcome to go ahead and try anyway.

If you fail, it says "Told you so. That's what you get for trying something new. Why didn't you listen to me? Go back to what you know. It's safe there."

If you succeed, the voice says nothing.

I've managed to minimise the self-talk now because I know that I'm CAPABLE of doing things that are just outside the hula hoop – they're out of my reach, but within my grasp. I know that logically, there's more chance of me succeeding than failing, and I'm willing to accept that what happens if I fail isn't the end of the world.

But when I start doing things that are well outside my comfort zone – that's when my inner voice starts shouting from the rooftops:

"What the hell do you think you're doing?"

"What are people going to think of you?"

"You're not good/clever/smart/fit/good-looking enough for that"

I started podcasting, and filming live videos on Facebook towards the end of 2016 – two things that were very much new to me, and absolutely miles outside of my comfort zone. I'd spent the best part of two decades at this point sat in my bedroom office, quietly getting on with building and investing in businesses. Pointing a camera at me, switching on a microphone, and saying "right John, educate and entertain these people for the next 25 minutes" was pretty bloody scary.

And low and behold, the self-talk returned. I knew I had to combat it, and I knew that it's all a load of rubbish, that my subconscious is talking to me in order to persuade me to stay exactly where I am, and not to risk trying anything new.

I'd be sat there some days, watching the countdown before we went live on Facebook.

3...

2...

1...

And I'd be thinking to myself for those three seconds "You're going to mess this up, You're going to stumble over your words. Who the hell are you to talk on this subject anyway? There are people who have degrees in this stuff, guys who've written books on it. Why the hell is anyone going to listen to YOU?"

That's a lot of thinking to cram into three seconds. It's probably why it took me 10 to 15 minutes every time to build up the courage to actually press the "Go Live" button which starts the countdown.

For the average 40 minute podcast, I'd spend around two hours researching, writing the script, and making sure that everything flowed properly. A bit of post-production, keeping on top of comments, and on average one episode of the Big Idea Podcast would take me four hours. I'd finish the episode on a high, think it had gone really well, only to see that we'd had five or six live viewers on Facebook.

Cue that bloody voice in my head again...

"No-one's listening. Nobody cares. You're wasting your time. Don't bother carrying on with it. Quit now before people REALLY start laughing at you for your pathetic attempts at it. You're no 'expert', and people can see right through you."

And then two days later, I'd get an email from someone who'd watched the video, and they'd say something like "Thanks for your latest video – I found it really inspiring, and I did X, Y, and Z as a result of what you taught me".

Take that, self-talk!

Real comments, from real people are far more valuable feedback than the negative BS that your own mind will feed you in order to keep you within your comfort zone. Yet as humans, we tend to forget the nice things that people say about us, and only remember the horrible, negative things that someone once said, or more often, that we say about ourselves.

 BIG IDEA...

You can't shut the voice in your head off, but you can PROVE it wrong. The more you prove it wrong, the QUIETER it gets.

It was the positive comments from real people that kept me going, and yet it remains (and still is) a battle between the real people telling me that they loved what I was doing, and my self-confidence which was telling me that everyone else hated it.

I spoke to one of my mentors around this time, who is a fellow podcaster, and who was around a year ahead of me in his podcasting career, yet who seemed light years ahead in terms of his popularity. I was struggling to get 100 subscribers, and he had 100,000. I asked him how I could turn off this damaging self-talk?

"You can't. I still get it now. Sure, I've got 100,000 subscribers, but Tim Ferriss has got three million."

His self-talk is very similar to mine, only the numbers on the barometer are different. What we're both doing wrong is comparing our Page 17 with someone else's Page 294. It's not even the same book. We're not comparing apples with apples – we're comparing apples with pianos.

I was having a wobble after doing 12 episodes. He'd done over a hundred, so was much more relaxed, and in his stride about it. But then, he'd compare himself to Tim Ferriss who'd been doing it for three years longer than him, who had far better contacts than him, and who had done twice as many episodes.

So I'm none the wiser as to how you switch off that self-talk, other than to say that everyone gets it. All you can do is battle through it, prove that voice wrong – and the more it's proven wrong, the less it'll have to say in the future. It really does happen to everyone. You're not alone. I'll bet even Donald Trump has MOMENTS – just fleeting moments when he has a niggle of self-doubt, and wonders whether he's qualified to do something. Or maybe he's the one exception, and a warning to the rest of us about what happens if you DON'T have that little voice in your head...

1,000 true fans

The conversation I had with that fellow podcaster really opened my eyes, and I realised that I was chasing these huge numbers which actually meant nothing to me. I didn't need 100,000 subscribers. I was doing this to "scratch an itch" – to do something that I was passionate about, not just to earn a few quid from it. I didn't need 100,000 or a million people to like what I do – I needed 12 people to LOVE what I do – enough that they'd part with money to work with me.

 BIG IDEA...

You don't need EVERYONE to like you.

It's better to mean a great deal to a small number of people than to mean little to a great number of people. Have a read of Kevin Kelly's essay "1,000 true fans" which describes this principle better than I could ever hope to:

http://kk.org/thetechnium/1000-true-fans/

If everyone seems to love you, remember you don't have the Midas touch. You're not that good.

If everyone seems to hate you, remember it's nothing personal. You're not that bad.

You're just you. There's no-one else like you. Go be you.

SO... WHAT NOW?

"If you trust in yourself. . .and believe in your dreams. . .and follow your star. . . you'll still get beaten by people who spent their time working hard and learning things and weren't so lazy."

Terry Pratchett, The Wee Free Men

STOP...

Stop right now.

Yes, you're very nearly at the end of this book – but I don't want you to do what MOST people do when they're reading the final chapter of a personal development book. I don't want you to think to yourself "Tick! That's another book read. I can't wait for my life to automatically improve just as a result of reading it. Now, which one shall I read next?"

What do you want to be DIFFERENT as a result of reading these last few hundred pages?

What's going to actually CHANGE in your life after reading this book?

If the answer is "nothing", then you've wasted your money buying it, you've wasted your time reading it, and you'll keep on wasting time and money reading book after book after book until you start taking... ACTION.

 BIG IDEA...

DON'T put down this book until you've decided what you're going to IMPLEMENT.

Remember the five magic ingredients

1. GOALS. Set a "North Star" goal, and work backwards from there. What needs to happen in five years' time to be on track for it? What about 12 months from now? What about 90 days from now? One month? Next week? Tomorrow?

2. DESIRE. Nothing happens unless you truly want it badly enough – everything has a price. Desire is the price you're willing to pay.

3. KNOWLEDGE. What you put in your mouth affects your health. What you put in your head affects your wealth.

4. ENVIRONMENT. Your network equals your net worth. Who you hang around with matters. What you read, watch, and listen to matters – more than you could ever know.

5. ACTION! The most magical of all the magic ingredients. Nothing happens – absolutely nothing changes until you actually take ACTION!

Put the five ingredients together, and you've got a recipe for success. Set some nice clear GOALS, ones that will stretch you. Make sure they're aligned with what you truly DESIRE, and that you're willing to do what's necessary to make them a reality. Get the KNOWLEDGE you need – the blueprints from those who've done it before, the road maps from your mentors. Make sure your ENVIRONMENT is congruent with what you want to achieve. And then there's only one thing left to do...

Make it happen

Take the actions that you KNOW you need to – when you need to. Keep on track, get someone to hold you accountable, and watch the magic happen.

 BIG IDEA...

Remember, nothing happens without ACTION – regular, habitual work on the RIGHT THINGS.

The life you're currently living, and the lifestyle you're currently enjoying is the result of the choices you have made, and the actions you have taken thus far. Sure, you can blame it on the government, your parents, your teachers, your upbringing, your friends and family. You can even blame it on Brexit, or Donald Trump. But the fact remains that you can't control ANY of those things. The only thing you can control is how you REACT to them, and the actions that you take on a daily basis.

Set yourself clear goals, and align those goals with what you truly desire. As Arnie says: "If you have a clear vision of where you want to go, the rest of it is much easier... you know why you are training five hours a day, why you're going through the pain barrier, why you have to eat more, struggle more and why you have to be more disciplined"

10x results don't have to come from 10x effort. The small things, done consistently, add up to be BIG things. Just start rolling that snowball down the hill. Remember that this doesn't have to happen overnight. It's the culmination of focusing on the right things on a daily basis for a prolonged period of time that makes special things happen. When I said in 2001 that I wanted to "have a real business one day", I had no idea that I'd be in the position I am right now – I simply couldn't comprehend the journey from where I was then to where I am now. All I could do was put one foot in front of the other – and now, here I am!

 BIG IDEA...

No matter where you are in your life right now, START rolling your snowball down the hill.

I'm a normal bloke – nothing special

Yet I've earned a couple of million quid building dodgy looking websites on the internet . Those people who you're holding up on a pedestal as an example of "success" are also just normal blokes and girls. They've all got flaws, weaknesses, chinks in their armour that make them no better than you or I – but they've learnt that when life deals you a good hand, you go all in. They've learned to maximise one or two elements of their character that are their strengths.

I haven't been dealt a Full House. But I've got a pretty decent hand – maybe three twos? But whatever hand YOU'VE been dealt, it's not your job to moan and bitch about it – it's your duty, your responsibility, to max out what you HAVE been given, and make the most of the cards you've got to play.

Let go of what's not working, and go "all in" on what is working – your ONE thing.

I was at a conference recently, at which Gary Vaynerchuk was due to deliver a keynote speech. For the majority of the two-day event, my fellow attendees were the usual British crowd – reserved, polite clapping in all the right places, tutting and rolling their eyes during the thinly-veiled sales pitches– you know the score.

And then Gary Vee arrived, and those same blokes in suits, who had quietly sat and taken notes for two whole days suddenly turned into thirteen-year-old girls,* mobbing Gary the minute he arrived at the venue, trying to touch him, shake his hand, grab a selfie with him – Screams of "We love you Gary", and "Gary, you rock!" could be heard all around us, as the organisers pumped up the music, turned on the smoke machine and disco lights, whipping the entire crowd into a frenzy to "make some mother-f***ing noise for Gary Vaynerchuk!"

(* Just the way I would have too, if it had been Warren Buffett delivering the keynote...)

As far as Rock Star Business coaches go, Gary Vee's one of the biggest stars – it's why he was able to command a six-figure fee for what was effectively a 45 minute Q&A session. But he's just a normal bloke. No, really he is. Sure, he runs a $100m company, has over 1.5m followers on Twitter, and his YouTube videos have been watched more than 30 million times.

But he's just a normal guy like you and me, who's figured out what his strengths are, and he plays to them.

Don't believe me?

Head to YouTube, and search for "Wine Library TV Episode 1" – where you'll be greeted by a nervous looking bloke with bad hair, sat in a dingy-looking room with a few bottles of wine in front of him. The lighting is bad, the video production is amateur, and the presenter, a down-to-earth guy who introduces himself as the "Director of Operations at WineLibrary.com", looks like he'd rather be anywhere else than in front of the camera.

BIG IDEA...

DON'T put anyone on a PEDESTAL. If they did it, so can you.

That video was shot in 2006.

That bloke was Gary Vaynerchuk.

Watch that video, and tell me that you couldn't do what that ordinary bloke did with a shaky camera, a YouTube account, and bad hair, back in 2006. Stop comparing his page 399 with your page 4.

Most of those business superheroes that you worship are nothing of the sort – they're just ordinary people like you and me.

Sometimes they're willing to do what others are not

If you're preparing for a marathon, this could be as simple as training on a cold, rainy Sunday morning, or Christmas Day – just doing what your competitors are not willing to do gives you an immediate competitive advantage, and – just like the Team GB men's Eights rowing team from Sydney 2000 – ask yourself how you can make YOUR boat go faster?

Also remember to ask yourself WHY you want your boat to go faster in the first place. What's the big picture? What's it all for? Which end of the see-saw are you sat on right now? Don't be like Robin Williams, chasing success after success, and yet eventually dying unhappy and unfulfilled. Turn off the TV, look after your health, and start living a life that's true to you. Get a team of superstars to support you – there's no such thing as a self-made man. Everyone who's had any level of success has done so through the hard work, skill and determination of many, many people – even if they THINK they've done it all on their own!

Stop beating yourself up, and stop believing your own hype. You're not THAT good. But you're not THAT bad either. Stop letting fear control your life and restrict your growth. Do something every day that's just outside your comfort zone. Grow that hula hoop every single day.

Focus

Really focus, on the ONE THING that's going to make ALL the difference. The thing that if it were the ONLY thing you accomplished today, you'd be able to call it a good day of progress towards your goals.

Block out the time to work on your ONE THING. And protect that time with your life. Anyone stopping you from doing your ONE THING is stealing the food from your children's mouths. Don't let them!

Ready to start the magic?

Goals... Check.

Desire... Check.

Knowledge... Check.

Environment... Check.

Action...?

GO... DO...

NOW!

ARE YOU READY TO JOIN THE ONE PERCENT?

"Having a mentor is a brain to pick, an ear to listen, and a push in the right direction."

John C Crosby

99% of small business owners aren't currently living the lifestyle they want.

They're working harder than they want to, for less money that they want.

They don't enjoy their work, and they don't get to spend quality time with their family.

The idea of taking a fortnight out of the business to go on holiday fills them with dread in terms of whether there'd actually be a business for them to come back to.

Does this sound familiar to you?

If this sounds like your situation, and the lifestyle you're currently "enjoying" isn't what you dreamt it would be when you first started your business, then I've got three rather stark facts for you:

1. It's YOUR fault
2. You CAN do something about it
3. We can HELP you

That's why I created the One Percent Club. Over the last few years, I've helped hundreds of small business owners design their business around the lifestyle that they want.

That means different things to different people – some may want to earn £100k a year, others to spend more time with friends and family.

You may want to travel the world, or plan your retirement for ten, five or maybe even two years' time. Maybe you want to remove yourself from doing the jobs you hate, for clients you also hate?

Or perhaps you want to give up your day job, or shut down one business to focus on the business you're really passionate about?

Whatever the lifestyle YOU want to design, we can help you become the architect for it – drawing up the plans, and turning your dreams into reality.

Don't get me wrong – YOU'LL still be doing all the work. This isn't business growth by abdication! What the One Percent Club will do for you is to give you CLARITY on what your ONE THING should be, and to hold you ACCOUNTABLE to make sure you bloody well do what you say you're going to do.

We only take on TWELVE new One Percenters every 90 days, so there is an application process.

If you go to http://www.bigidea.co.uk/opcc-book, you can join the waiting list for the next intake.

When the doors are open, we'll provisionally allocate places to the first 12 people who apply, on a first-come-first-served basis. But we'll want to speak to you before confirming your place, as we want to make sure that you're the right person to become a One Percenter – if you're not willing to change, not flexible about trying new things, not open to new ideas and different ways of thinking, then I wouldn't bother applying – but then you probably wouldn't have made it to the end of this book if you were that sort of person!

 BIG IDEA...

Working with mentors gives you CLARITY about what you should be focusing on, and ACCOUNTABILITY to make sure it happens.

OPCC members will get:

- "My World Domination Plans (Volume I)" – the actual planning tools that I've used to increase my business eightfold over the last five years.
- Direct access to me, Jason, Rob and the entire Big Idea team
- A weekly online meetup, giving you some "virtual" face-to-face time with us, and your fellow One Percenters
- Unlimited marketing critiques
- Your own accountability partner
- Your own private Facebook group, just for One Percenters
- You'll learn everything that I learn.

We'll work with you to distill that massive list of everything that you COULD do, into just three BIG things that will make a difference to your business, and to your lifestyle, in the next 90 days.

We'll then make bloody sure you actually DO those three things, and help you with the "baby steps" along the way to achieving those three biggies.

 BIG IDEA...

MENTORS are there to give you help and advice, a shoulder to cry on, and a kick up the arse, depending on what you need at the time!

Ready to join the One Percent, and have John and Jason working with YOUR business?

Go to http://www.bigidea.co.uk/opcc-book to join the VIP waiting list today (remember we only accept 12 new OPCC members every 90 days).

What do people say about working with John and Jason?

"Without John's support I wouldn't have taken the plunge and be where I am today. John taught me that there's no point setting a target unless it's ambitious – and there's no point in being ambitious unless it's achievable. The goals that I have achieved through the One Percent Club, even helped me to win an all-expenses paid ski trip with my family."

Dave Clewer
Mortgage Advice Bureau

"John and Jason have been there and done it and don't have an ego about it like many others. I know I am better organised, better planned and prepared and more likely to succeed sooner, thanks to their wisdom and experience."

Matt Tricot
1upsearch

"John and Jason are the real deal, they've been there and done that. I know that. And that equips them more than almost anybody else to speak about what they do with such authority and knowledge."

Dave Stickland
The Store Guru

"I joined the One Percent Club to hold me accountable. I have thousands of ideas – and so I need someone like John to reign me in and focus on just one thing. John is down to earth and genuine. He's so motivated! He has a positive outlook, and certainly doesn't take any nonsense. I need to start looking at expanding – taking it to the next level, and I'm glad John is there to help drive my business forward."

Jo Lines
Ambition Property Group

"We all run out of willpower at one point or another but John adds that accountability into the mix and makes it happen. John is always achieving, you are always fighting to keep up. His lifestyle is pretty admirable – he takes pretty long holidays and that's something that is important to me. Just being around him is infectious; all these excuses that you would normally make – you can't do with John!

You sit in a conversation with most people and tell them 'how hard' things are – but with John he doesn't accept it. He just says 'why don't you do that?'. There's no argument. It's great!

He is an everyday guy but living the life he wants to live, where he wants to live it. He gets to pay good attention to his family and friends. He doesn't have to work 22 hours a day and I admire him for that. John's marketing skills are second to none. He has a really actionable approach to everything which is what makes him so great to work with."

Andy Carr
The Renovation Men

WANT MY HELP... FOR FREE?

"Free education is abundant, all over the internet . It's the desire to learn that's scarce."

Naval Ravikant

Are you a small business owner who likes to think BIG but don't have the budget to stretch to paid-for mentoring just yet? Then my FREE Facebook group, "Ambitious. Lifestyle. Business." is for YOU.

www.bigidea.co.uk/facebook

It's a place where AMBITIOUS business owners learn and share SIM-PLE, PRACTICAL tips and advice to help their businesses GROW with ONE purpose... TO PROVIDE THEM WITH THE LIFESTYLE THEY WANT. Whatever that means for YOU... Maybe you want to earn £100k a year?

Maybe you want to spend more time with friends and family, or travel?

You might want to give up the day job, or completely change direction in your business.

Perhaps you want to retire in X years? Remove yourself from doing the jobs you HATE?

Sack your problem clients?

The group is 100% FREE. There are no ads.

No spammy upsells.

No fluffy, woo-woo BS.

Just simple, practical help to grow YOUR Ambitious Lifestyle Business.

WHAT DO WE DO IN A.L.B?

1. LIVE WEEKLY PODCAST. Every Monday lunchtime, Jason and I record the latest episode of the Big Idea Podcast. And you get to watch the LIVE recording, including an exclusive Q&A afterwards just for you guys.

2. LIVE INBETWEENISODES. A week is too long to wait, so I'll quite often grab my phone, or turn on my webcam and start yacking – there's usually a simple, practical business tip or something inspirational in each one.

3. HELP. We're here for YOU. Whatever you need help with – if we can help you, we WILL. If we can't help you, we'll usually be able to find someone who CAN. You just have to ASK. Myself, Jason, Matt and Rob are in the group every single day of the week, so post whatever's on your mind, and let's get you doing the RIGHT shit in your business.

4. NETWORK. We're not trying to build the biggest small business group on Facebook here. We're trying to build the best. And that means we're really picky about who we let in (and who we let stay in to be honest!), but it also means that we've got a really high calibre of "experts" on hand.

Whether you want someone who knows SEO, analytics, mindset, copywriting, Facebook ads, LinkedIn, video production, funnel building, or Professional Dicking About On Facebook, there'll either be someone BLOODY GOOD in the group, or someone in the group will have that person in THEIR network.

They say that "Your network equals your net worth." That means that by joining this group (and crucially by ACTIVELY PARTICIPATING in it), you've just increased your net worth – Good Work!

5. ACCOUNTABILITY. We're here when you need a shoulder to cry on. But we're also here (and dare I say famous for!) giving people a kick up the arse when they need it. Tell us what you're going to do, and then DO IT... We'll hold your feet to the fire and make SURE you do it, and accept no excuses for failing to do what needs to be done.

What are you waiting for? Visit:
www.bigidea.co.uk/facebook

ABOUT THE AUTHOR...

"When I write, I feel like an armless, legless man with a crayon in his mouth."

Kurt Vonnegut

John Lamerton is a serial entrepreneur and investor, a former civil servant, who started a dotcom company back in 2000, despite having no skills, knowledge or experience – "but then neither did most of the other dotcom businesses at that time, so I was in good company!"

He's owned a website that told students where to get free sachets of shampoo, one that told people they'd been caught speeding (when they hadn't!), and one that told football fans where to get the best pies.

Before he knew it, he was running a dating website, selling office space, working with florists to sell online, and selling package holidays to the Algarve. He's also owned a bingo website, a finance blog, sold mobile phone insurance, and streamed live sports events.

Trust me, that's the short version too – John's owned and operated more than 100 different websites since that first one in 2000. Most have been either sold, or closed down, and he now works primarily in three sectors:

SPORTS BETTING. John owns a number of online sports betting brands, and specialises in building large, loyal communities of sports betting fans. He's always looking to add to his portfolio, so if you know of any sports betting communities that are looking for a new home, please get in touch – john@bigidea.co.uk

MENTORING. John's main passion these days is mentoring ambitious, lifestyle business owners. John runs a paid group mentoring program (the One Percent Club), as well as a FREE Facebook group, which can be found at: www.bigidea.co.uk/facebook

INVESTING. John invests in UK property, both residential and commercial, as well as providing angel investment to some of his mentoring clients. He also buys large, established websites, particularly in the sports betting sector.

He's a perennial optimist, firmly believing that the mighty Plymouth Argyle will one day play in the top-tier of English football. So far though, he's witnessed four promotions and five relegations. Still, it only takes a couple of back-to-back promotions...

He lives in Plymouth with his wife Sarah, and two children, Jack and Harry.

He's also a bit of a fanboy of Warren Buffett.

And he can always, ALWAYS be bribed with cake.

Mmm, cake...

Photo credit: John Lamerton

26418221R00137

Printed in Poland
by Amazon Fulfillment
Poland Sp. z o.o., Wrocław